BETWEEN

THE DUNGEON

AND

THE LIGHT

B·E·T·W·E·E·N

THE DUNGEON

AND

THE LIGHT

CHOOSING VALUES FOR A BRIGHTER FUTURE

JOHN WESLEY FOWLER

REVIEW AND HERALD® PUBLISHING ASSOCIATION
HAGERSTOWN, MD 21740

The author assumes full responsibility for the accuracy of all facts and
quotations as cited in this book.

Texts credited to NIV are from the *Holy Bible, New International Version.*
Copyright © 1973, 1978, 1984, International Bible Society. Used by
permission of Zondervan Bible Publishers.
Texts credited to NKJV are from The New King James Version. Copyright © 1979,
1980, 1982, Thomas Nelson, Inc., Publishers.
Bible texts credited to Phillips are from J. B. Phillips: *The New Testament in
Modern English,* Revised Edition. © J. B. Phillips 1958, 1960, 1972. Used by
permission of Macmillan Publishing Co., Inc.
Bible texts credited to RSV are from the Revised Standard Version of the Bible,
copyright © 1946, 1952, 1971, by the Division of Christian Education of the
National Council of the Churches of Christ in the U.S.A. Used by permission.

This book was
Edited by Gerald Wheeler
Cover designed by Willie S. Duke
Typeset: 13/14 Bernhard Modern

PRINTED IN U.S.A.

01 00 99 98 97   10 9 8 7 6 5 4 3 2 1

R&H Cataloging Service
Fowler, John Wesley, 1935-
    Between the dungeon and the light.

    1. Apologetics.   I. Title.

            239.7

ISBN 0-8280-1069-2

· C O N T E N T S ·

•ACKNOWLEDGMENTS•

Wishing to give credit to the many people who had provided help in editing and polishing his manuscript, one author began his acknowledgment with the following: "This book comes to publication trailing clouds of the kindness of others."

Only a writer and those who assist him or her know the taxing hours of tedious yet rewarding effort that go into writing a book, or the hours of wide reading and disciplined thought necessary to gain the inspiration that gives life and body to such an effort. Writing during one's off-hours compounds the challenge. My warmest gratitude goes to Kay, my wife, who suffered through my silence as I wrestled with the plethora of ideas considered and then patiently typed and retyped the manuscript on her off-hours.

Jeris Bragan deserves special note for the encouragement and skilled editorial help he freely gave me. But most important, Jeris urged me to move away from a heavy scholarly approach in writing to one that "maintains the scholar's focused, critical, analytical eye for detail, mingled with the artist's eye for colorful description and clobbering quotations, then wraps the package up in the lively, forceful, and prophetic voice that demands a hearing." I'm not sure I approximated that lofty ideal.

My heartfelt thanks to those who critiqued the manuscript, making helpful suggestions that most always I edited into the manuscript. Especially motivating was Clifford Goldstein's phone call, after he had read a first draft of the manuscript, encouraging me to persist in the effort and offering to write a letter of recommendation.

• I N T R O D U C T I O N •

The oft-seen murals of the ancient Greek actor's masks portraying comedy and tragedy well depict the future that confronts twenty-first-century humanity. Scientific progress seems to offer unbounded health and happiness. My scientist son-in-law believes that one day medical science, using genetic engineering, will discover how to correct the damaged or malfunctioning genes that cause sickness and death. However, these same sciences also crack open a door to the worst atrocities and suffering imaginable, worse than those perpetrated either by Nazism or Communism.

Consequently, all branches of knowledge are rushing feverishly to find answers to life's moral, ethical, and scientific questions—answers that might guide modern humanity as it moves inexorably into a promising yet frightening new world. Where did human beings come from? Why are we here? and What is our future? are questions that we must answer.

The world's greatest minds are hard at work seeking those answers. What we need is a framework in which science, philosophy, and theology can cooperate to find the answers to these fundamental questions. Many feel that an evolutionary worldview best provides that framework. However, others seriously question whether that perspective is adequate.

This book addresses these pressing issues. It divides into three major sections. The first endeavors to describe the muddle of modern thought and why it has failed. The second section attempts to develop a Christian apologetic expressed in logical and reasonable propositions that avoid obsolete jargon, unjustifiable assumptions, and unsound arguments. The third section seeks to show how Christian faith is relevant to the individual, to society, and to a world in crisis.

THE MUDDLE
OF MODERN THOUGHT

THE DUNGEON OF UNBELIEF

———◆———

THE "KINGDOM OF GOD" IS THE OVERRIDING BIBLICAL SYMBOL FOR THE FUTURE. IT INDICATES THAT THE FUNDAMENTAL SHAPE OF THE FUTURE IS TO BE DEFINED PO-LITICALLY. THE WORD "KINGDOM" IS THE FUNDAMENTAL METAPHOR BY WHICH THE BIBLICAL TRADITION UNDERSTANDS HUMAN SOCIAL DESTINY.[1] THE POSITION IS ROOTED IN AN ETHIC THAT HAS FULL CONFIDENCE IN THE ABILITY OF MAN TECHNICALLY AND POLITICALLY TO SHAPE HIS DESTINY.[2]
——MAX L. STACKHOUSE

FEW PEOPLE EVER CRACK OPEN A TEXT IN LOGIC, AND MATCHING THEIR DISIN-TEREST IN THIS DISCIPLINE, THEY DEVELOP A CONTEMPT FOR ANY USE OF LOGIC BY ANYONE WHO CHALLENGES THEIR ILLOGIC. IT IS UNDERSTANDABLE WHY TEXTBOOKS IN LOGIC DO NOT HIT THE BEST-SELLER LIST, BUT THE LAWS OF LOGIC MUST APPLY TO REALITY, ELSE WE MAY AS WELL BE LIVING IN A MADHOUSE.[3]
——RAVI ZACHARIAS

Between episodes of trancelike silence, the 35-year-old woman struggles sporadically against the restraints binding her arms and legs. They protect her and the hospital staff from injury when her unpredictable psychotic rage explodes. Brown hair, streaked with premature gray, mats against her sweaty forehead.

It's hard to believe this confused and terrified woman stretched out on the bed is also a highly educated professor of philosophy at a major university. Only days earlier she was teaching graduate students how to think about life.

Now her once-distinguished face is drawn into a paranoid scowl, and her eyes, unfocused and frantic, dart about the room, searching, peering owlishly at some invisible object.

Suddenly a new sound, a chilling cackle, gurgles in her throat. She raises her head off the sweat-soaked pillow, her eyes fixated on the small gold cross pinned to the pastor's lapel. A cunning gleam in her eyes, she whispers in a barely audible, conspiratorial voice. At first the words are almost incoherent. A flash of lucid rationality interrupts her unintelligible muttering. "We're all dead, you know," she says in a perfectly ordinary tone of voice.

Then the singsong chant returns, her voice rising and falling as though she were singing a favorite nursery rhyme from her childhood. "God is dead. You are dead. I am dead. We're all dead . . . dead . . . dead . . . dead . . . dead!"

Her chilling chant reminds me of Nietzsche's madman, who on a bright morning lights a lantern and rushes through the marketplace screaming, "God is dead! God is dead! And we have killed Him."[4]

The thrashing woman's voice grows louder, changes pitch. She begins to sing, in a mournful, disjointed chant, fragments of a popular song by Peggy Lee that suggests that if life has no meaning, one might as well get totally drunk. At last she falls silent and stares at the ceiling.

Pity. A brilliant mind broken by the most destructive and deadly curse of the nuclear age: the demon of doubt, the dungeon of unbelief. She is trapped in the utter despair of a hopeless and meaningless existence.

Something has destroyed the faith, hope, and meaningful existence of millions of people today. While many do not express their despair as graphically as this philosophy professor, they live lives just as empty, just as painful. Why has this plague of meaninglessness swept the world?

For most people this century began with a profound sense of hope and optimism. But something unexpected happened in the midst of Western humanity's optimistic march into a brave new world—the twentieth century exhausted itself in an unrelenting orgy of self-destruction.

Hope and optimism vanished like smoke before the wind. Deprived of its spiritual roots, a confused and sick society stumbles down the dangerous path toward a culture of death as the twentieth century staggers to a close.

Even a casual glance at the world around us confirms this. Consider the disintegration of the family. One out of every two marriages ends in divorce. Fathers abandon their children, while single mothers with dependent children—the fastest-growing poverty group in America—struggle to survive. Battered wives, abused children, latchkey kids, child violence, gangs, and rape and sexual assaults testify to a world shattering apart. Political greed, a legacy of massive public debt for our grandchildren, corruption in the business world, and talk show depravity undermine every social institution.

There's more.

Consider the frightening environmental destruction perpetrated by virtually every nation under the sun: dying rain forests; depletion of the ozone layer and its resulting skin cancer epidemic; petrochemical poisoning of water and air; the growing threat of new Chernobles; the devastation of marine life.

The cry of Nietzsche's madman and the despairing lyrics of Peggy Lee sung by a psychotic philosophy professor vividly describe the frightening reality that confronts our daily lives. Dead or alive, God is irrelevant, many believe, and human existence has absolutely no meaning, purpose, or direction.

How did this happen?

ENLIGHTENMENT TURNS OUT THE LIGHT

Paradoxically, the first tiny seeds of our contemporary existential despair sprouted 200 years ago in the dawn of the Enlightenment. Emerging ideas, like ravenous rodents, chewed away at the very foundation of Christian culture until its internal structure collapsed.

The Enlightenment sought to account for the whole of life strictly within the bounds of natural reason. It understandably rejected a world of superstition and inexplicable forces. But it was not content to stop there. It made the human mind the measure of *all* things. Thinkers assumed they could understand and explain everything about reality, and began to cast loose from all external and objective authorities. Humanistic ideas that made finite humanity the final arbiter of right and wrong replaced all external and objective authorities. People began to apply the scientific method of study and research to all branches of knowledge, including the religious and spiritual realm. The rejection of biblical realities followed, which allowed the evolutionary worldview to gain dominance, and intellectual thought gradually denied any supernatural activity in the origin and development of life on our planet. Millions, like Nietzsche, jumped to the conclusion that there is no personal God. If they couldn't understand or prove His existence, then He must not exist at all. Thousands of others, even professing Christians, while not denying the reality of God, relegated Him to the sidelines of daily life.

Recent research shows that while 90 percent of Americans claim to believe in God, their religion plays virtually no role in their decision-making, their moral or sex lives, their family relationships, or their relationship with others. "In every single region of the country, when we [surveyors] asked how people make up their minds on issues of right and wrong, we found that they simply do not turn to God or religion to help them decide about the seminal or moral issues of the day."[5]

Western society has dethroned religious reason, rejecting the lofty role it has played in the past. Disillusioned by the failure of Enlightenment ideas to create the expected utopia, modern philosophy has abandoned any effort to develop a unified system of thought that would explain life in a wholistic and meaningful way. Consequently, scientists, scholars, and theologians tend to emphasize specific areas of knowledge, resulting in a fragmentation of philosophy and theology. This, in combination with an existential approach to reality, gave birth to relativism and pluralism, which cut humanity loose from objective truth, further undermining faith in spiritual realities.

The result? There are no absolutes, and everything is relative. My way is as good as yours. If it feels good, do it. What I do is nobody else's business. Every person becomes his or her own authority. Research reveals that only 13 percent of Americans believe in fixed moral laws such as the Ten Commandments.[6]

Rejecting the past, modern thought tends to turn reality on its head and to reconstruct history to undergird its view of how things should be. We see reconstructionism at work in popular movies, such as *Dances With Wolves* and Oliver Stone's *JFK*. The conflict over the proposed Smithsonian display depicting Japan as an innocent victim in the bombing of Hiroshima and Nagasaki is still another example of historical reconstructionism.

Much of Christianity, in partnership with modern thought, has yielded its belief in absolute truth. Many denominations have jettisoned the moral authority of the church and the Bible. Since we can no longer trust past claims to absolute truth, modern thought, including much of Christianity, operates from an almost entirely pragmatic agenda. If we have no way of knowing objectively what is right or wrong, then whatever works, whatever satisfies, whatever appeals, has to be right.

Consequently, what we once considered basic moral principles all become void. Crime is a disease, and criminals, being simply a product of time and place and circumstance, are no longer responsible for what they do. Someone else is. Everything can be justified in terms of environment, biology, or chemistry.

When Eric and Lyle Menendez were asked their reason for the bloody shotgun slaying of their parents, they replied, "We couldn't take their abuse any longer." Incredibly, the legal system is often buying these ludicrous arguments. Juries are showing a willingness to place responsibility for a wide spectrum of crimes on one's environment, body chemistry, or biology.

But human beings are not animals. Meaning, as Dr. Viktor Frankl has so brilliantly documented from his experiences in the Nazi death camps and the psychiatrist's couch, is found in one's belief system and one's faithfulness to that system.

Show me a person who is emotionally ill or who exhibits criminal behavior, and I'll show you a person whose fundamental belief system is all mixed up. People with such problems experience too much cognitive dissonance in their belief system, or they live lives contrary to their fundamental beliefs.

INTO DUNGEONS OF DEATH

Whenever people sever the connection between themselves and their spiritual roots, they invariably find themselves cast adrift in a world that suddenly has little sense of meaning, purpose, or direction. Their selfish needs of the moment begin to dictate their behavior.

The time-tested laws of the Judeo-Christian tradition prove that even in this unbelieving age there are ways that might seem right, but that in the end bring only disillusionment, sorrow, suffering, and death.

The pitiful deathbed testimony of Thomas Paine, the renowned American author and infidel, graphically validates this truth. "I would give worlds," he gasped, "if I had them, that *Age of Reason* had not been

17

published. O Lord, help me! Christ, help me! O God, what have I done to suffer so much? But there is no God! But if there should be, what will become of me hereafter? Stay with me, for God's sake! Send even a child to stay with me, for it is hell to be alone. If ever the devil had an agent, I have been that one."[7]

Such blindness to ultimate reality is a perfectly logical consequence of restricting one's beliefs to just what we can see in this world. Thomas Carlyle has shrewdly observed: "A person who doesn't habitually worship is but a pair of spectacles behind which there is no eye."

No one is exempt from this blindness so long as he or she ignores the spiritual realities that confront all of humanity. Millions blinded by a warped belief system grope about in the darkness, seeking meaning in vivid personal experiences, drugs, promiscuous and deviant sex, and other forms of psychological Russian roulette. Yet the sought-for reality turns out to be only an illusion.

Augustine declares that humanity was made for God, and we are restless until we find rest in Him. How did Augustine know this? He learned it the hard way: by a painful personal experience that almost broke his mother's heart and nearly destroyed his chances of ever finding meaning and purpose.

Perhaps Nietzsche caught a distant glimpse of our time and recognized the mischief that his ideas would create when he observed: "The death of hope leads to the hope for death." Paradoxically, Nietzsche himself fell captive to this death of hope. Meaning and purpose eluded him throughout his life. In the end he became insane, and he spent the last years of his life under the care of his mother, whose faith in God he had spurned.

People who cut themselves off from their spiritual heritage function about as well as a car fueled with maple sugar. It may seem sweet for a while, but you're not going anywhere. No matter how much you like maple sugar, your Toyota won't run on it; and no human being functions in any fully human, fully alive sense while in denial of his or her basic human condition.

While Eden's freedom beckons mockingly from a distant shore, a heartless world slowly strangles all joy, hope, or courage. We live in an increasingly violent culture in which security and fulfillment elude us, in which nothing really counts, and in which life becomes a rotten absurdity.

Lee Iacocca expressed this absurdity when he wrote in his book *Talking Straight,* "Here I am in the twilight years of my life, still wondering what it's all about. . . . I can tell you this, fame and fortune is for the birds."[8] Jack Higgins, author of *The Eagle Has Landed,* had something very similar to say: "When you get to the top, there's nothing there."[9]

Or is there?

---

[1] Max L. Stackhouse, *Ethics and the Urban Ethos* (Boston: Beacon Press, 1972), p. 99.

[2] *Ibid.,* p. 37.

[3] Ravi Zacharias, *Can Man Live Without God?* (Dallas: Word Publishing, 1994), p. 11.

[4] Richard John Newhouse, in *First Things,* April 1994, p. 59. Friedrich Nietzsche was the father of modernism.

[5] James Patterson and Peter Kim, *The Day America Told the Truth* (New York: Prentice Hall, 1991), p. 199.

[6] *Ibid.,* p. 6.

[7] Quoted in Herbert Lockyer, *Last Words of Saints and Sinners* (Grand Rapids: Kregel Publications, 1969), p. 132.

[8] Lee Iacocca and Sonny Kleinfield, *Talking Straight* (New York: Bantam Books, 1989), p. 33.

[9] Quoted in Alister McGrath, *Intellectuals Don't Need God* (Grand Rapids: Zondervan Pub. Assn., 1993), p. 15.

TRUTH OR CONSEQUENCES?

IN 1933 THE BAVARIAN MINISTER OF EDUCATION, MR. SCHEMM, DECLARED SOLEMNLY BEFORE THE ASSEMBLED PROFESSORS OF THE UNIVERSITY: "FROM THIS DAY ON, YOU WILL NO LONGER HAVE TO EXAMINE WHETHER SOMETHING IS TRUE OR NOT, BUT EXCLUSIVELY WHETHER OR NOT IT CORRESPONDS TO NAZI IDEOLOGY." [1]

—DIETRICH VON HILDEBRAND

TO CHOOSE ONE'S VICTIM, TO PREPARE ONE'S PLANS MINUTELY, TO STAKE AN IM-PLACABLE VENGEANCE, AND THEN TO GO TO BED . . . THERE IS NOTHING SWEETER IN THE WORLD. [2]

—JOSEPH STALIN

Executioner Blokhin, armed with a whole suitcase full of Walther 2 German revolvers, said to the 30 other Russian soldiers with him, "Come on, let's go."

It was 1940, and the Russian Army had just occupied Poland. Their assignment was to execute 6,000 young, well-educated Polish Army officers being held in a prison camp near Kalinin, Poland. They were only a part of the 15,000 Polish officers Russia eventually killed. Stalin saw them as a potential danger, as enemies in advance.

Blokhin, the primary executioner, put on his leather hat, brown leather apron, and long brown leather gloves, which reached above the elbows—an outfit that had become his executioner's uniform and his trademark. Then he and three other Russian soldiers led the Polish officers one by one to the restroom for the prison staff. They asked each man his surname, first name, and place of birth. In order to hide what was happening from the rest of the Polish officers, each Polish officer was blindfolded and led to a soundproof room next to the restroom where he was shot in the back of the head at close range.

Three hundred unsuspecting Polish officers died in the darkness of the first night. The leather uniform served its purpose well, as the blood of 300 men splashed and splattered over everything in the room, including the man doing the killing. Finding it too taxing to kill 300 men per night, Blokhin reduced the number to 250. He and his men spent the entire month of April murdering the 6,000 unsuspecting Polish soldiers.

A pragmatic application of the ideas of Karl Marx had led to the killing of the Polish officers. When discovered, these grisly murders opened a small but chilling window on the evil nature of the most costly experiment in social engineering human history has ever witnessed. The gang of thugs who called themselves the Communist Party was eventually to imprison, torture, and murder millions of people.

Ideas and concepts have consequences—good and bad! And there appears to be a bundle of bad ideas circulating today.

Here's the pagan mantra, rooted in the dominant ideas of our time and chanted by millions:

There is no objective truth.

There are no absolutes.

All values are relative.

One idea is as good as another.

This life is all there is, so grab all the gusto you can.

It doesn't matter what you believe as long as you believe something.

On the surface they may sound perfectly rational and even liberating. Who could object intelligently to such superficially benevolent ideas? Isn't tolerance in the marketplace of ideas one of the great virtues?

Actually, the muddle-headed tolerance of some ideas reflects an inability to think clearly in terms of cause and effect, because every idea, whether good or evil, has predictable consequences!

There's only one thing wrong with any of the "new" ideas described above: these anti-Christian, anti-Bible ideas lead to death. Moreover, these ideas aren't as new as you might think. In fact, they're subtle variations on a very ancient theme.

The powerful appeal of the idea the serpent presented to Eve in Eden was virtually irresistible. The serpent's promise that Adam and Eve would not die created the certainty that human beings would die.

Who says that ideas don't matter?

A basic fact of human psychology states that we do what we are, and we are what we believe. That simply means that what we do, how we function and behave as humans within our families and communities, reflects what we really are as a person. Furthermore, what we are as persons, whether courageous or cowardly, generous or stingy, loving or hateful, has direct roots in what we believe about human origins, God, and the meaning of life. Reality is not necessarily what we say we believe, but what we honestly do believe behind our words, pretensions, and facades.

To put it another way, what we truly believe eventually shows up in our behavior. You can't live crooked and think straight. Neither can you think crooked and live straight. "For as [a man] thinketh in his heart, so is he" (Prov. 23:7).

Individuals who say, for example, that they "believe" in a loving, merciful, gracious, redemptive God but shoot abortion doctors, are hostile toward the marginalized and oppressed, and root for the death penalty as if it were a circus event live at their roots incongruent lives, and the fruit of their lives, regardless of their pretensions, wreak havoc on society. Research shows that the problems plaguing the Christian world are little different from those destroying the happiness of non-Christians.

Dishonesty, sexual promiscuity, deviant sex, sexual abuse of children, divorce, greed, and religious illiteracy and indifference—all are the common lot of both Christians and non-Christians. Sadly, few professing Christians seek the guidance that their religious teachings offer. What is even more revealing is that most church members don't even know their own church's position on the important issues confronting the church and society.[3]

What we believe to be true or false ultimately becomes our convictions. That's critically important, because beliefs and convictions about anything lead eventually to direct consequences in our behavior. To put it another way, every idea you hold that is solid enough to lead to a conviction has predictable cause-and-effect consequences that will evolve into concrete behavior over a period of time.

Jerry Plecki, a Chicago schoolteacher, believes that dishonesty must be a way of life. That idea led him to give his students the answer keys for a national academic testing competition. When asked by a student how he could justify his actions, he replied, "Everybody cheats. That's the way the world works."[4] Ideas obviously have consequences. When the public learned of his actions, he resigned his teaching job.

A DOMINATING IDEA

Here's another idea that has come to dominate our culture: human existence and every other aspect of life as we know it are nothing more than the accidental by-products of infinite space plus infinite time plus an infinite number of random chances—a reasonably fair description of the basic idea of evolution. It's just an idea; it is no more an irrefutably proven fact than the ideas found in the Genesis account of Creation are irrefutable facts. But it can be tested against reality.

Belief in an evolutionary origin of flight, for example, offers one critical test case of evolution. Current evolutionary theory says that the ability to fly evolved separately and independently four different times—in insects, birds, mammals, and reptiles. In each case it is supposed to have taken millions of years, requiring almost innumerable transitional forms. But science has not found a single example of an evolutionary transitional stage.[5] In addition, while science has some evidence that can be interpreted to support evolutionary origin of flight, it does not have one shred of factual proof that it actually did happen.

But it is an idea with consequences, and in time people begin to behave toward one another as if it were true. A person who really believes that another person is a cosmic by-product of space, time, and chance will treat that individual accordingly. He or she will use, manipulate, exploit, or abuse that person to get whatever he or she wants.

Ideas, once they burrow into the fabric of any society, can have draconian consequences. Sexually transmitted diseases are the by-product of ideas that promote the "new morality." The murder of unborn children becomes nothing more than a personal approach to birth control.

Evolution has such frightening consequences simply because it obscures the reality of a personal God. With its concept of a developing future utopia, evolution gave birth to the utopianism of Bolshevism, which in turn led to the modern totalitarian state. Stalin's goal was to assist the evolutionary process in creating "the new man," which would in turn create the new utopian society and world. Mikhail Suslov, one of the leaders of the plot to overthrow the Communist system, claimed: "The Communist Party of the Soviet Union proceeds and has always proceeded from the premise that the formation of the new man is the most important component of the entire task of the Communist construction."[6]

Thus it was not difficult for Stalin to decide to employ the so-called law of natural selection, which called for the survival of only the fittest, in his efforts to create his "new man" and his utopia. It enabled this ruthless dictator to find sweet sleep after he had planned for the killing of his enemies—20 million of them, including hundreds of his own friends and whoever else got in his way.

When someone asked Solzhenitsyn how Communism could brutally put so many millions of people to death, he answered simply, "We have forgotten God."

When human beings throw off the discipline of revealed truth, their freedom ends in slavery. Religious tyranny must, of course, be abhorred, but when humanity uses its coveted freedom to ignore God, an even worse tyranny follows: one dramatically illustrated by the death camps of Hitler and the vengeful purges of Stalin.

If our existence is merely an absurd flicker of light between two eternal darknesses, then life has no real meaning, purpose, point, or direction. All is random chaos operating under a thin veneer of self-serving civility—when it's convenient. As a consequence, no individual has any inherent worth beyond sex appeal, wealth, or power. When marriage no longer serves a spouse's selfish purposes, divorce often quickly follows.

Still other ideas have surfaced that suggest that maybe people have always existed somewhere in space and that perhaps our ancestors came here on a spaceship from somewhere, and . . . and . . . and . . . But after exploring all theories about origins, one is left either with the idea that life began by chance or some superior power or being started it all.

Furthermore, these two main approaches get complicated by being mingled with existentialism, which says that how we feel about a thing is all that is important, and by determinism, which claims that everything is fixed by unalterable natural law.

So what difference does it all make? Isn't one idea just as good as another?

Actually, at the risk of sounding confrontational, I believe that such relativism reflects a lack of disciplined, rational thinking. Every idea that leads to beliefs or convictions (here we go again!) has consequences for good or ill. Furthermore, if we don't have some reasonable process by which people can reach general agreement about "good" versus "bad" ideas, then words like truth, beauty, etc., are essentially meaningless concepts.

If, for example, the word "green" can mean any color on the spectrum, depending on your subjective preference, then the color green is a meaningless word that describes nothing.

Since ideas have observable consequences, a culture dominated by evolution shouldn't be surprised at what the concept has led to.

AN IDEA WITH A NEW TWIST

The Christian church, bloated and spiritually sluggish itself, easily fell prey to the so-called scientific ideas. It was all too eager to please and prove itself intellectually acceptable to those forces that were, in fact, uncompromisingly hostile toward many traditional Christian beliefs. Unable to rouse itself to respond to the challenges of many of the new ideas and concepts, it allowed itself to be coopted by anti-Christian forces.

A so-called scientific method of study preempted the unique Christian approach to the discovery of truth. Instead of forcing empirical reality into the clearly defined interpretive framework of the past, scientists and theologians could now allow empirical data to lead where they would, even if the data seemed to undermine the conventions and truths of the past. Science and theology, which were once a handmaiden of morality, then became an ally of agnosticism.

Many theologians, for example, linked the ideas of special creation and evolution into a concept labeled "theistic evolution." Today there appears to be an almost universal acceptance of such a scientific worldview among evangelical theologians. Zachery Hayes, a leading contemporary theologian, in his stimulating book *What Are They Saying About Creation?* said recently: "At the present time it would be true to say that some form of evolutionary theory is found to be acceptable to the mainstream of theologians and the major Christian traditions of the West."[7]

25

Theistic evolution clouds the concept of a personal God and usu-ally leads to a pantheistic view of the Deity. God becomes a quasiper-sonal force in nature, while godlike powers are attributed to the impersonal forces of nature. This pagan idea shoves God to the side and views life as a creation of the capricious laws of nature. Even the most ethereal parts of life that once seemed heaven-sent science now explains to have natural causes. Love itself—mother for child, hus-band for wife, sibling for sibling—some scientists now attribute solely to a chemical called oxytocin. How do we know? Because researchers have found that rats cuddle when injected with this chemical.[8]

Consequently, some go overboard with the fact that emotions and thinking have a biochemical base and reduce human beings to nothing more than D-base protoplasm, as one popular biologist put it, and love is nothing more than biology and chemistry propped up by illusions, romantic or otherwise. A hand may paint a work of art, but that work of art is more than muscle and bone. It had a creative mind behind it.

To treat human beings as nothing more than chemistry quickly leads to dangerous consequences. Within such reasoning, marriage has no ultimate, transcending meaning or purpose, at least not beyond mundane contractual law. If your husband or wife, for example, exists only as an accidental by-product of random events, what rational value does this person have intrinsically in his or her personhood? How is she or he anything more than a babymaking, pleasure-producing "piece of meat"—even with the vulgar qualification of a "fine piece of meat"?

So fathers merrily abandon their children and wives. And women, having discovered they have the right to be just as cynically self-absorbed as some men, are rapidly catching up in their own self-centered behavior.

One woman who was influenced by this idea went for a job inter-view during her honeymoon. She met a man she fancied more than her new husband. Immediately she divorced her husband and married the new acquaintance. When asked why she walked away so quickly from her first marriage, she responded, "I know it sounds shocking, but there are times in your life when you just have to go after what you want."

When we lose the concept of a personal God, self-centeredness takes over and personal gratification becomes the number one goal. As a consequence, the family becomes another business, with marriages

26

treated like business mergers and divorces like divestitures.

Who wins in this self-serving world? Someone said that it's "the person who dies with the most toys."

Theological liberalism adopted "scientific" methods of criticism to the point that it reduced God and the supernatural to the level of only what the human mind can conceive of. It succeeded in gutting the historical Christian faith to the point where the sacred became the silly.

Too many of the clergy sought popularity with the unchurched by shaving away at the edges of anything that dared to confront the world. Instead, the church increasingly offered what some theologians eventually dubbed "hot-tub religion," a feel-good, self-indulgent gospel presided over by a cheerful, good-natured grandpa God who demands nothing in terms of personal commitment, sacrifice, or righteousness. The success of the hot-tub religion's mission is measured exclusively in terms of church growth. Transformed lives are irrelevant. Looking good is more important than being good.

Today this mingling of an uncompromising secular humanism and a compromised Christianity has spawned a new paganism that has become the dominant and dominating worldview of our time. We need only to look backward to the fourth century and the time of Constantine to discover where these age-old ideas will once again lead us.

This illustrious yet pagan Roman ruler transformed a church that had survived persecution into an oppressive institution that gloried only in power and prestige. Nothing could stand in the way of its desire for glory and power. Few contest the fact that the church of the Middle Ages killed at least 50 million Christians.

And make no mistake about it, pagan worldviews almost totally dominate our culture. All too often the body of Christ embraces this baptized paganism. Consequently, it speaks in a fractured and disjointed voice. The church timidly turns the other cheek and attempts peaceful, nonconfrontational coexistence with an increasingly hostile world that bluntly rejects the God of Creation and ridicules the revelation of Scripture.

Without the direction and discipline available only in Christian truth, Western culture, awash in a religion of flabby sentimentality, cut loose from its biblical roots, now drifts meaninglessly toward nowhere. Carl F. Henry describes Western society as "intellectually uncapped, morally unzipped, and volitionally uncurbed."[9]

Contemporary religious thought so misrepresents the nature and character of God that one might as well believe that either God does not exist or He has lost interest in human affairs. Liberal Christianity has become little more than window dressing on a very old paganism. And liberal Christianity is not alone in its denial of biblical truth. Some forms of "conservative" Christianity are no more biblical than their liberal counterparts. They too lust for popularity, political power, the status quo, while showing indifference to the oppressed and marginalized.

Whatever religious ideas they may hold today, very few believe God has much, if anything, to do with our daily lives. Egocentric human beings strut into the spotlight of center stage. A sick and twisted narcissism explodes into an orgy of crime and chaos.

Again we ask ourselves, Do ideas have consequences? You bet they do! And so do Christian ideas. However, rather than bringing enslavement and death as does the new paganism, I believe I can show that the teaching of Christ offers life and freedom.

---

[1] Detrich von Hildebrand, *The New Tower of Babel* (Manchester, N.H.: Sophia Institute Press, 1953), p. 52.

[2] In M. Lincoln Schuster, *The World's Great Letters* (New York: Simon and Schuster, 1940), p. 495.

[3] See J. Patterson and P. Kim, *The Day America Told the Truth*, pp. 75, 142, 143, 199, 200, 237.

[4] *Newsweek,* Apr. 10, 1995, p. 19.

[5] Colin Mitchell, *The Case for Creationism* (Grantham, England: Autumn House, 1994), p. 131.

[6] Quoted in David Remnik, *Lenin's Tomb* (New York: Random House, 1993), p. 31.

[7] Zachery Hayes, *What Are They Saying About Creation?* (Maywah, N.J.: Paulist Press, 1980), p. 53.

[8] Robert Wright, "Science, God and Man," *Time,* Dec. 28, 1992, p. 40.

[9] Quoted in *Current Thoughts and Trends* 10, No. 10 (October 1994) : 7.

HUMANITY'S SEARCH FOR MEANING

WITHIN THE HUMAN EXPERIENCE, THE HUNGER FOR MEANING IN EACH SUCCEED-
ING GENERATION IS NEITHER DIMINISHED NOR DISPELLED, SCIENTIFIC ADVANCES AND
NEW PSYCHOLOGICAL OR SOCIAL THEORIES NOTWITHSTANDING. WHAT BEST EXPLAINS
THIS HUNGER FOR MEANING? AND HOW CAN IT BE SATISFIED?[1]
—RAVI ZACHARIAS

HE WHO HAS A WHY TO LIVE FOR CAN BEAR WITH ALMOST ANY HOW.
—FRIEDRICH NIETZSCHE

The smell of burning flesh permeated the air as the trains disgorged their human cargo at Auschwitz, the German death camp that has become a household word and symbol of all evil throughout the world. The smartly uniformed guards carefully eyed the prisoners as they tumbled out of the trains. They told the Jews to leave their luggage and fall into two lines, the men on one side and the women on the other. As the lines of humanity filed past the SS officer, he raised his right hand and with the forefinger pointed either to the right or the left, indicated which direction each person should turn. Ninety percent veered to the left. These, who were judged not physically fit, went straight to the crematorium. The others marched to the work camps.

"Detachment, forward march! Left-two-three-four! Left-two-three-four! Left-two-three-four! Left-two-three-four! First man about, left and left and left and left! Caps off."[2] Auschwitz's most renowned inmate, Viktor Frankl, author of the widely circulated book *Man's Search for Meaning*, remembered those commands from a Nazi guard the rest of his life.

Anyone who did not march properly got a kick. The prisoners

stumbled on in the darkness, over big stones and through large puddles, along the one road to the camp. The accompanying guards kept shouting at them, driving them with the butts of their rifles. The tired and weak supported themselves on companions' arms. Hardly anyone spoke a word. The icy wind discouraged talk. Hiding his mouth behind his upturned collar, the man marching next to Frankl whispered quietly, "If our wives could see us now! I do hope they are better off in their camps and don't know what is happening to us."[3]

The man's comment awakened thoughts of Frankl's own wife. As the two men stumbled on for miles, slipping on icy spots, supporting each other time and again, dragging one another up and onward, they said nothing, but they both knew they were each thinking of their wives. Weariness, exhaustion, discouragement, hopelessness, and fear dogged their steps.

The men knew death waited for the weak in the holster of the guard.

As they struggled along, Frankl's mind clung to the memory of his wife. He seemed to see her smile, her frank and encouraging look. The sense of her presence was real. The treasure of her love gave him a reason for clinging to life.

Later he eloquently expressed that transcendent moment and the meaning it brought.

"For the first time in my life I saw the truth . . . that love is the ultimate and the highest goal to which man can aspire. Then I grasped the meaning of the greatest secret that human poetry and human thought and belief have to impart: The salvation of man is through love and in love. I understood how a man who has nothing left in this world still may know bliss, be it only for a brief moment, in the contemplation of his beloved. In a position of utter desolation, when man cannot express himself in positive action . . . man can through loving contemplation of the image he carries of his beloved, achieve fulfillment."[4]

If nothing else, history has taught us the necessity of finding meaning and purpose in life. Even though Nietzsche was so wrong in most of what he said, his idea about the importance of meaning was right: If we have a why to live, we can bear with almost any how.

The ultimate consequence of a life without meaning is that we have nothing worth living for. And it follows that without purpose nothing is worth dying for. Meaninglessness will eventually paralyze even the most sincere individual. The person with little meaning in life quickly gets jumpy, jittery, acts crazy, goes to pieces.

E. Stanley Jones tells of seeing a man stagger through a railway station in Japan with a huge carton on his bent back. The carton contained the words "The Universe."[5] That burdened man graphically portrays modern humanity. Television, newspapers, radio, books, and magazines dump the "universe" and its troubles on the backs of old and young alike. A weary meaninglessness sucks out our energy and drags us down.

A cynical young man asked a professor of history, "What's your racket?"

The professor replied that he was a historian, and then he asked the young man, "Aren't you interested in history?"

"Naw," he replied, "I'm willing to let bygones be bygones."[6] Nothing interested him. For him, as for millions of others, life held little meaning or purpose.

FINDING MEANING AND PURPOSE

There are many ways to find meaning in life. Frankl's experience demonstrated that to love and to be loved can bring a great deal of purpose to life. A challenging career can fill a life with significance. Frankl identifies three essential ways to find meaning: "By doing a deed, by experiencing a value, and by suffering."[7]

However, we can find ultimate meaning only in an understanding of the transcendent purposes of life, both in the present and in a future life after death. And only religious teachings can bring us that ultimate understanding and certainty. Paul Tillich has noted that religion involves that which concerns us ultimately. Religious teachings answer ultimate questions by explaining our origin, nature, and destiny. Second, religious teachings enable us to interpret positively the experiences that befall humanity, both individually and collectively, thus bringing sense and significance out of them.

Even though condemned to life in prison for a crime to which he pleaded not guilty, Jeris Bragan accepted the idea of the apostle Paul's that all things can work together for good. This enabled him to identify many blessings that evolved from his time in prison. The time behind bars gave him time to "study, think, and reflect on a variety of theological issues," which otherwise he would never have done. He experienced "the deepest fellowship with Christ, the greatest personal liberation" he had ever known. The uninterrupted seclusion gave him time to think and write. And finally, his high school sweetheart tracked him down in prison, where they were later married. Jeris states that the importance of her love in helping him cope with his tragic circumstances "would be impossible to overstate."[8]

Religion functions in the life of believers by explaining (1) the purpose of our existence, (2) the nature of reality, (3) the fate of the world, (4) the character of the supernatural beings or forces that determine our destiny, and (5) how we are to relate to those forces.[9]

Religious beliefs best answer those ultimate questions of life by explaining life's experiences in the context of a universe caught up in a conflict between good and evil, yet guided and controlled by divine forces.[10] Such an understanding of the universe, which we call a biblical or Christian worldview, most satisfactorily explains both the crises of our individual lives and those of our world.

Our faith in God, then, brings with it a system of beliefs and practices by which we struggle with the ultimate meaning and purpose of life. Such a belief system enables us to answer life's fundamental questions of life, thus establishing us in a faith-obedient relationship with God. Such a religion creates a meaningful and powerful spiritual experience both for us as individuals and for the church collectively.

However, apart from the Christian worldview, meaning and its offspring, hope, have escaped us. A speech by the great scientist Stephen Hawking highlights the hopelessness of the non-Christian. Severely impaired by amyotrophic lateral sclerosis (Lou Gehrig's disease) and able to speak only through a speech synthesizer, Hawking said that because of the weaknesses of the evolutionary process, our long-term survival and any hope for our species are in question. However, he added, "If we can keep from destroying each other for the next 100 years, sufficient technology will have been developed to distribute humanity to various planets, and then no one tragedy or atrocity will eradicate us all at the same time."[11]

CAN MAN LIVE WITHOUT MEANING?
Can we learn to live with ambiguity, confusion, and meaningless-

ness? Both theology and sociology argue that human beings must have a sense of significance and purpose. Someone has said that we are "meaningmongers," that is, we are beings that are oriented to meaning. It is a human characteristic to ask why. We sense with the psalmist that our years should be more than a "tale that is told." They must have meaning and purpose.

The ultimate threat to individuals, to society, and to the church is the danger of meaninglessness. If anything destroys our system of belief and practice, we cannot maintain our spiritual life. When life is void of meaning, faith fades, hope dies, and we cease to struggle. What is left? In the words of a simple sonnet: "My days are in the yellow leaf, the flower and fruit of love are gone; the worm, the canker, and the grief, are mine alone."

Viktor Frankl records a dramatic demonstration of the close link between the loss of meaning and death. His senior block warden, a fairly well-known composer and librettist, confided in him, "I would like to tell you something, Doctor. I have had a strange dream. A voice told me that I could wish for something, that I should only say what I wanted to know, and all my questions would be answered. What do you think I asked? That I would like to know when the war would be over for me. You know what I mean, Doctor—for me! I wanted to know when we, when our camp, would be liberated and our sufferings come to an end."[12]

"And when did you have this dream?" Frankl asked.

"In February 1945." (It was then the beginning of March.)

"What did your dream voice answer?"

Furtively he whispered to Frankl, "March 30."[13]

When his friend told Frankl about his dream, he was still full of hope and certain that the prophecy would be fulfilled. But as the thirtieth of March drew nearer, they knew that they would not be free on the promised date. Toward the end of March the man lost all hope. On March 29 he suddenly became ill and ran a high temperature. Then on March 30, the day his prophecy had told him that the war and suffering would be over for him, he became delirious and lost consciousness. The next day he died.

THE POWER OF MEANING AND PURPOSE

Conversely, if people can understand why bad things befall them, if they can see their problems within the context of a large, long-range good, a broader cosmic and divine purpose, they can overcome them, or at least learn to cope with them and go on to find peace, fulfillment, and achievement. Meaning and purpose enable us to face ridicule, discouragement, persecution, and even death itself.

Meaning and purpose have historically and repeatedly changed people's lives for the better. They have been the antidote for discouragement, the rehabilitator of criminals, the rescuer of alcoholics, the deliverer of drug addicts, the preventer of suicide, the cure for many psychosomatic disabilities, and the solution to many cases of poverty, failure, and despair. When people see themselves as a part of cosmic purpose or plan, when they believe that "all things work together for good," nothing can discourage or dissuade them. The meaning they find in their religious faith enables them to rise above whatever challenges, however difficult, life presents to them.

Condemned to die at the stake, Catalan Girard, a leader of the Protestant Vaudois churches in the Piedmont valleys of southern France during the sixteenth century, exhibited no fear as the flames leaped up around him.

Standing at the stake, within scorching flames, he asked for two stones, which someone quickly fetched for him. In the midst of the consuming flames, hands still tied, barely allowing him to rub the stones together, he said, "You think to extinguish our poor churches by your persecutions. You can no more do so than I with my feeble hands can crush these stones."[14] Not the torture of the flaming stake nor the fear of death itself could persuade this man of faith to reject that which gave his life meaning and purpose.

A CLEAR AND PRESENT DANGER

However, today modern forces seek to undermine the religious teachings that give meaning and purpose to life. Karen Armstrong, a contemporary critic of the Christian faith, believes that Christian beliefs are nothing more than a creation of the human mind. Scornfully, she argues that "only Western Christianity makes a song and dance about creeds and beliefs."[15] If Christian truths are not trustworthy, then Armstrong is correct, and the claims of Christianity are simply "a song and dance." Nothing more!

Many have come to believe just that. Relativism and anything-goes pluralism undermine all absolutes and argue that we have no right to disagree with those of differing views. Respecting only openness, this fluffy-headed tolerance includes every point of view except those perspectives that do not include every point of view! It is tolerance only for those who march in step with the tolerant crowd. Few comprehend the incipient meaninglessness lurking in such shadowy reality.

Many use this uncritical tolerance as an excuse for perpetual skepticism that effectively keeps any religious commitment at arm's length. It also opens a doorway for the most bizarre ideas. The frightening scenarios of Jim Jones and David Koresh graphically illustrate this clear and present danger. Knowable truth, we are told, might exist in mathematics and science, but not in religion or morality.[16]

But logic, reason, history, and reality resoundingly refute such shallow claims. "For anyone to take seriously the statement that there is no truth that corresponds to reality defeats the statement itself by implying that it is not reflective of reality. If a statement is not reflective of reality, why take it seriously? Truth as a category must exist even while one is denying its existence and truth must also afford the possibility of being known."[17]

Many argue that only Christianity claims the exclusive right to truth. However, every religious system is implicitly exclusivistic. Buddhism, Hinduism, and Islam each present themselves as the only system of religious beliefs that pulls everything together into a universal system able to answer the ultimate questions of life adequately.

Pluralism claims that all theological truth claims are conjectural. However, if all truth claims are conjectural, then pluralism, being a truth claim, is also itself conjectural. Yet pluralism condemns all who do not accept a pluralistic view of truth. By its own standards, pluralism stands condemned.

Why then should Christianity be scorned or ridiculed because of its notion of truth as absolute. Truth, by definition, will always be exclusive. Most would agree that Jesus claimed exclusivity. The real question, as Zacharias points out, "is whether Jesus' claims to truth can pass the tests for truth, and whether in His Person He meets those tests."[18]

Ravi Zacharias suggests three tests to which we should subject any system or statement that makes a claim to truth. Those tests are: (1)

logical consistency in what is stated, (2) empirical adequacy in which its truth-claims can be tested, and (3) experiential relevance, that is, whether it applies meaningfully to a person's life.[19]

This book aims to show that Christianity passes these tests with flying colors.

THE PRESENT CHALLENGE

Today many insist that Christian beliefs are nothing more than a song and dance, a matter of personal taste. However, claims prove nothing. Instead, experience proves that Christ can answer the ultimate questions of life. A truthful knowledge of Him does bring unprecedented meaning and purpose into our lives. The convincing evidence undergirding the unique power of Christian faith is open to investigation. We can lay its life-giving roots bare for all to see.

A skeptical Lew Wallace, a well-known writer in the late nineteenth century, determined to put Christianity's truth to test. He researched the life and teachings of Christ and the apostles. What he found made him a believer, resulting in the best-seller *Ben-Hur* and a life of devotion to Christ and His church.

I invite you to join me as we search for satisfying answers to the urgent questions that trouble our generation. Our goal is to find the ultimate meaning and purpose of life. I hope to revive that so-called song and dance about Christian creeds and beliefs. Come along as we stir up powerful and convincing arguments—arguments consistent with the laws of logic and reason—that seek to prove the validity of the claims of the Christian faith about God, His nature, His work, and His character.

We shall see that the Christian faith offers reasonable and meaningful answers to the urgent questions we struggle with—where we came from, why we exist, and what our future is. The task before us is that of justifying the extraordinary claim of Christianity, the exclusivity and uniqueness of Jesus Christ.

Larry King, television talk-show host, made a very perceptive comment when someone asked which past historical figures would he have most liked to interview on his show. One of those he mentioned was Jesus Christ. When questioned why Christ, he replied, "I would like to ask Him if He was indeed virgin born, because the answer to that question would define history."[20]

Larry King easily identified the central question of every philosophical and theological pursuit. If Jesus is what He claimed to be, then the truth-claims of Christianity are valid, and Christianity alone offers to humanity the answers to all of life's ultimate questions, and consequently, it alone brings to us ultimate meaning and purpose.

Today some still agree with Karen Armstrong's statement that Christian beliefs are nothing more than "a song and dance." They also echo Nietzsche when he wrote, "You caged God, tamed Him, domesticated Him, and the priests pliantly lent their aid. The roaring bull has become a listless ox. You have gilded God."[21]

Come along as we prove both Nietzsche and Armstrong wrong!

[1] R. Zacharias, *Can Man Live Without God?* (Dallas: Word Publishing, 1994), p. xvii.

[2] Viktor E. Frankl, *Man's Search for Meaning* (New York: Pocket Books, 1963), p. 57.

[3] *Ibid.*, p. 58.

[4] *Ibid.*, pp. 58, 59.

[5] E. Stanley Jones, *Conversion* (Nashville: Abingdon, 1959), p. 19.

[6] *Ibid.*

[7] Frankl, p. 176.

[8] Jeris Bragan, *When You Walk Through a Storm* (Boise, Idaho: Pacific Press Pub. Assn., 1991), pp. 43, 44.

[9] Dean Kelley, *Why Conservative Churches Are Growing* (New York: Harper and Row, 1972), p. 38.

[10] Peter Berger, *The Sacred Canopy* (Garden City, N.Y.: Doubleday and Company, Inc., 1967), p. 117.

[11] Quoted in R. Zacharias, *Can Man Live Without God?* p. 170.

[12] Frankl, pp. 119, 120.

[13] *Ibid.*

[14] J. A. Wylie, *History of the Waldenses* (Mountain View, Calif.: Pacific Press Pub. Assn., 1977), p. 65.

[15] Karen Armstrong, *A History of God* (New York: Random House, 1993). Quoted in *Time*, Sept. 27, 1993, p. 77.

[16] Erwin W. Lutzer, *Christ Among Other Gods* (Chicago: Moody, 1994), p. 30.

[17] Zacharias, p. 125.

[18] *Ibid.*, p. 126.

[19] *Ibid.*, pp. 123, 124.

[20] In Zacharias, p. xviii.

[21] Harry Cox, *Religion in the Secular City: Toward a Postmodern Theology* (New York: Simon and Schuster, 1984), p. 200.

A CHRISTIAN APOLOGETIC

CHAPTER 4

GOD AMONG OTHER GODS

IN HER BOOK "A HISTORY OF GOD" KAREN ARMSTRONG ARGUES THAT GOD IS IN-
DEED A PRODUCT OF MANKIND'S CREATIVE IMAGINATION. GOD, SHE SAYS, MAY WELL
BE OUR MOST INTERESTING IDEA. SHE CLAIMS THAT YAHWEH (HEBREW FOR JEHOVAH)
WAS ORIGINALLY A SAVAGE, PARTISAN GOD OF WAR AND ONE OF SEVERAL DEITIES
WORSHIPED BY THE ISRAELITES. IT TOOK SEVEN CENTURIES FOR THIS UNPLEASANT
BEING TO EVOLVE INTO THE ALMIGHTY YAHWEH PROCLAIMED BY THE PROPHETS AS
THE ONE AND ONLY GOD. NEW IDEAS ABOUT GOD HAVE ALWAYS EMERGED IN RE-
SPONSE TO NEW PSYCHOLOGICAL NEEDS. IN FACT, SHE THINKS THAT IF THE GREAT
FAITHS DID NOT HAVE THE CAPACITY TO CHANGE, THEY MIGHT WELL HAVE WITHERED
AWAY. CONSEQUENTLY, EACH GENERATION HAS TO CREATE ITS OWN IMAGINATIVE CON-
CEPTION OF GOD.[1]

—ERWIN W. LUTZER

I started to pray aloud, 'O Father,' and I stopped. 'O Brother,' and I
waited. And then I said, 'O ———.'" This "prayer" was spoken by
Susan Thistlethwaite, United Church of Christ professor of theology at Chicago Theological Seminary, in her conversion to femi-
nism.[2] It reveals something of the contemporary confusion about the
nature and character of God within late twentieth-century Christianity.

Barbara Lundblad, pastor of Our Savior's Atonement Lutheran
Church in New York City, attended some of the meetings of the
General Assembly of the Presbyterian Church (U.S.A.) during June
1994. After one meeting she announced euphorically, "Some authority would call our worship of last night verging on heresy. We did not
last night name the name of Jesus. Nor have we done anything in the
name of the Father, and of the Son, and of the Holy Spirit."[3] This particular meeting derided the Incarnation and the Trinity, contradicted
Scripture, and actively promoted a goddess named Sophia.

One speaker at this conference, Chung Hyun Kyung, revealed a blatant confusion about the nature of God when she described herself in the following words: "'My bowel is Shamanist, my heart is Buddhist, my right brain is Confucianist, and my left brain is Christian. . . .' Chung introduced her three special goddesses: Kali, the Hindu goddess of destruction; Quani, a Buddhist goddess who prays for the abolition of hell; and Enna, a Philippine earth goddess. 'These,' she exclaimed, 'are my new Trinity.'"[4]

James R. Edwards claims that a growing number of Christian denominations no longer have a single prevailing view of the nature of God. Syncretism, polytheism, pantheism, and monism are all in evidence.[5] For millions the God of Christianity is only one God among other gods.

Understanding the nature of God is pivotal in discovering transcendent meaning and purpose in our troubled world.

Few question the sincerity of the contemporary search for an understanding of God. Stephen Hawking, one of the world's most respected scientists, expresses the hope that someday humanity will "truly know the mind of God."[6]

Hawking's statement reflects the thinking of a significant number of contemporary scientists and philosophers. However, when Hawking speaks of God, he isn't talking about a personal deity. Like so many others, he has in mind an impersonal intelligence, or mind, at work in nature. He appears to agree with Karen Armstrong that the concept of a personal God is nothing more than an idea conjured up by the human creative imagination.

Wilbur M. Smith, a renowned author and lecturer, lamented as far back as 1961 that "not one in ten of the outstanding scientists of America believe in a personal God."[7] Smith quotes from a book written by 18 well-known American scientists, most of whom were teaching in our colleges and universities. The book attempted to set forth the concept of religion held by the 18 scientists. Smith writes that "not one of these scientists confesses that he believes in a personal sovereign omnipotent God, nor does one of them confess to any sure hope of personal life after death."[8]

WHAT OR WHO IS GOD?

The effort to develop a theology that brings meaning and purpose has always raised questions about the nature and character of this awesome reality and power that Rudolf Otto referred to as the "mysterium tremendum."

After the patriarch Jacob wrestled with this Being and was overcome, he asked, "Tell me, I pray thee, thy name" (Gen. 32:29). In other words: "Who are You?"

When God asked Moses to lead the children of Israel out of Egyptian bondage, he too had to have some answers. The question he asked underscored the difficulty of understanding this Presence or Person: "When I come unto the children of Israel, . . . and they shall say to me, What is his name? what shall I say unto them?" (Ex. 3:13).

While gazing up at the starry heavens, the prophet Isaiah sensed the presence of this mysterious Power or Being. His response evoked a similar question to that of Jacob and Moses: "To whom then will ye liken God? or what likeness will ye compare unto him?" (Isa. 40:18).

The essential question is What or who is God? In answer we must recognize that a full understanding of the nature and character of this Being we call God will always elude us. Yet the question's implications demand our attention. Whatever our belief or disbelief about God, few deny that those beliefs profoundly affect not only our view of life and the decisions we make, but our actions as well. Not a single aspect of our lives escapes the influence of our belief about God.

The effort to discover the nature of God comforts us with three basic options: theism; antitheism, or atheism; and pantheism. Theism views God as a personal being. Antitheism, or atheism, denies the existence of a personal God, and pantheism teaches that God is nothing more than an impersonal intelligence or force at work in the physical realm.

DEFINING ATHEISM

An antitheist, or atheist, is a person who maintains that there is no God; that is, that the sentence "God exists" expresses a false proposition. Atheism describes a person who rejects all belief in God.[9]

Ravi Zacharias makes a very revealing point when he argues that one arrives at atheism by default. "Atheism is not merely a passive unbelief in God but an assertive denial of the major claims of all varieties of theism; atheism contradicts belief in God while promoting a positive affirmation of matter as ultimate reality."[10]

Some take this approach to avoid having to defend their position, but it ends up denying the existence of God either implicitly or explicitly. Consequently, the atheistic belief statement is a totally unacceptable assumption because too often its proponent comes to it by default rather than by a logical or reasonable argument. Nazism, atheism's legitimate offspring, conceived by Nietzsche's atheistic philosophy, graphically illustrates its disastrous consequences.

Anyone who visits Auschwitz, as I did a few years ago, will have to face up to the evil growing out of an antitheistic worldview. Nothing has ever moved me more than seeing the building at this dark and foreboding death camp filled with human hair shaved from the heads of the victims just after they were gassed. A despairing sense of evil darkened my soul as I passed room after room filled with the jewelry, clothing, shoes, and even the eyeglasses stripped from the hapless Jews as they were dragged to the gas chambers and furnaces by antitheistic forces. Ravi Zacharias claims that documentation proves that the atheistic views of Nietzsche provided the rationale for Hitler's Holocaust.[11]

DEFINING PANTHEISM

Following hard on the heels of antitheistic science, much of the theological community began to accept an evolutionary worldview, with its pantheistic concept of God. C. S. Lewis wrote that "pantheists usually believe that God, so to speak, animates the universe as you animate your body: that the universe almost is God, so that if it did not exist He would not exist either, and anything you find in the universe is a part of God."[12]

Pantheism was the belief of the great Prussian philosopher Hegel, and I believe held today by many among Hinduism and Buddhism. The New Age religions proliferating in the land often hold to forms of pantheism.

What is pantheism? It comes from the word *pan*, meaning everything, and *theos*, meaning God. Pantheism means God in everything. In effect, God then becomes an impersonal intelligence and force intrinsic to nature itself. This intelligent force operates differently in the various pantheistic religions. Many of the New Age religions believe this force drives all life upward toward some distant utopia.

DEFINING THEISM

The Christian idea of God is reasonable and rational. The Greek word for God, *Theos,* gives us the term *theology,* the study of God. Theism identifies the teaching about God and is established not merely by intuition, but by evidence that appeals to logic and reason.

It pictures God as a personal being—a thinking, active, creative, supernatural person. We believe, as C. S. Lewis argues, that God invented and created the universe in a way that might be compared to the work of human beings today in making automobiles or houses or game parks. [13] An automobile is something distinct from the person who designed and made it. There is no logical basis for believing, for example, that a game park could make itself.

The teleological argument for the existence of God is an argument from design. The fact that we find a watch demands a watchmaker. If there is a world, there must be a God who made it. All of the basic arguments for God—the cosmological argument, the ontological argument, the historical argument, and the moral argument—appeal to logic and reason. Experience validates each approach.

After moving into my first district of churches as a young pastor, I quickly learned that I had inherited an alcoholic neighbor. He often visited with me, sharing the troubles—family, financial, and health—resulting from his addiction. One day my wife anxiously called me into the living room. There I found my drinking friend, who had pushed his way into our living room without even knocking, struggling with a chair to keep his balance. Pointing toward the living room window, he demanded, "Pastor, look out that window. Do you see that tree?" Pointing to a large oak tree just outside the window, he exclaimed, "Tell me, Pastor. Do you believe in God?" Without waiting for me to answer, he said, "That oak tree proves there is a God, doesn't it?"

His torrent of words rushed his argument. "Tell me, Pastor, does that oak tree have roots?"

"Yes," I replied, "that oak tree has roots."

"You are a man of God, so tell me, why are the roots of that oak tree underneath the ground, out of sight?"

"You tell me," I replied.

Without answering, he extended his question. "And why, Pastor, are the beautiful limbs and leaves of that tree above the ground where they can be seen?" Not waiting for me to answer, he made his point. "Because there is a God. God made that tree for us. If there were no God, the roots would probably be above the ground and the leaves underneath. Pastor, that tree proves there is a God, doesn't it?" His pleading voice trailed into silence as he slumped into the chair.

While his argument may have been a little simplistic, he legitimately appealed to logic and reason to support his tentative grasp on the reality we call God.

What does the Christian church mean when it refers to God as a personal being? Webster's dictionary defines *being* as existing or living.[14] The dictionary views the word *personal* as meaning a being or person who is rational.[15] The dictionary then defines God as a person or thing deified, a supernatural being, immortal, having power over people. *God* is a being who is "creator and ruler of the universe," eternal, infinite, all-powerful, and all-knowing.[16]

While the Christian view of God may be called an assumption, it is a logical and reasonable one based on good evidence.

NATURE SPEAKS TO US OF A PERSONAL GOD

The psalmist tells us that "the heavens declare the glory of God; and the firmament sheweth his handywork. Day unto day uttereth speech, and night unto night sheweth knowledge. There is no speech nor language, where their voice is not heard" (Ps. 119:1, 2).

Abraham Lincoln testified to nature's revelation of a personal God when he said: "I never behold them [the heavens filled with stars] that I do not feel that I am looking into the face of God. I can see how it might be possible for a man to look down upon the earth and be an atheist, but I cannot conceive how he could look up into the heavens and say there is no God"[17]

If we have ears to hear and eyes to see, nature will constantly speak to our senses of a personal and loving God. The responsive heart will see the love and glory of God through His created works. As one of my favorite authors said: "The green fields, the lofty trees, the buds and flowers, the passing cloud, the falling rain, the babbling brook, the glories of the heavens, speak to our hearts, and invite us to become acquainted with Him who made them all."[18]

JESUS REVEALED GOD AS A PERSONAL GOD

Jesus came to make God known. The apostle John declares that God has sent a message to us in Christ. That message is now that Jesus has come: "The darkness is past, and the true light [about God] now shineth" (1 John 2:8). Jesus Himself said: "No man knoweth who the Son is, but the Father; and who the Father is, but the Son, and he to whom the Son will reveal him" (Luke 10:22). When Jesus talked about going back to the Father, Philip said to Him, "Lord, shew us the Father" (John 14:8). Jesus' response makes the essential point that God the Father is like Him. He had come to reveal the Father: "Have I been so long time with you, and yet hast thou not known me, Philip? he that hath seen me hath seen the Father" (verse 9). The fact that Jesus was a personal being guarantees the personal nature of the Father.

Paul desired that every individual come to possess "the full riches of complete understanding, in order that they may know the mystery of God, namely, Christ, in whom are hidden all the treasures of wisdom and knowledge" (Col. 2:2, 3, NIV). While Paul speaks of hidden treasures, yet, as the whole passage implies, those treasures are no longer hidden, but brought to light. He offers the possibility of a full and correct understanding for everyone of the open mystery of God revealed in Jesus Christ.

The apostle Paul believed that "the light of the knowledge of the glory of God [shines] in the face of Jesus Christ" (2 Cor. 4:6). The life and teachings of Jesus present a perfect revelation of God. It lifts us above mere human speculation, thus enabling us to see and know the true and living God.

There is nothing in God's nature that we don't find present in Christ. Nothing that we can ever learn about God will contradict what we have seen or heard in Jesus. In Him dwells all "the fullness of the Godhead." This phrase, "the fullness of the Godhead," tells us that everything God is, every characteristic of deity—love, wisdom, authority, dignity, power, energy used to uphold and guide the universe—Jesus Christ has them all. When we have seen Christ, we have seen the Father (John 14:6). Jesus Christ brings into visibility the reality of a personal God with attributes that we as human beings can know. In Christ we can know that personal God and trust our lives to Him with an absolute certainty and assurance that He is willing and able to care for our every need.

Jesus used many illustrations that speak eloquently of God as a personal being. He spoke of God as being like a landowner who leased an orchard to evil people who killed the landowner's servants and son to get the property. However, the landowner, God, came and destroyed the evil men. How more personal can you get? He referred to God as a just judge who made sure that justice was done on behalf of His people. Jesus depicted God as a heavenly Father who notices even the sparrow that falls, and if He does that, certainly He watches over His children.

Jesus' life demonstrated His belief in a personal God. Often He openly spoke to His Father and made it clear that His Father spoke to Him. The two of Them carried on a conversation between Themselves. Jesus claimed to have been with the Father throughout eternity. He said that He had come from the Father and would go back to Him. Claiming that He did nothing but the Father's will, He prayed to the Father for help throughout His ministry, particularly in the Garden of Gethsemane just before the cross.

In fact, Jesus Himself claimed to be God and one of the members of the Godhead. He portrayed Himself as having been with the heavenly Father throughout eternity, and that He had come to earth to reveal this personal God. After suffering on the cross for us, He was raised from the dead and ascended into heaven, where He is carrying on a special priestly ministry at the right hand of the Father.

The point is that God is a personal God and that He is like Jesus. Why is He called the invisible God (1 Tim. 1:17)? Simply because it would be impossible for sinful human beings to look upon His shining brightness without being destroyed (1 Tim. 6:16; 2 Thess. 1:9). If we cannot gaze at the sun without damaging our sight, how can we expect to look upon the Being who not only made the sun, but walks up and down in its fire?

THE TRINITY: A PROFOUND MYSTERY

While many believe in God, few believe in a personal God. They feel that the mysterious something behind all other things must be more than a personal Being. Christians agree. But only Christianity offers any idea of what a being that is both personal and yet beyond personality could be like.

Equally hard to understand is the omnipresence of God. How can

48

God be everywhere at one and the same time? It is difficult for the human mind to wrestle with this difficult concept without denying the personhood of God and concluding, as do the pantheists, that God is only an intelligent force inherent in nature. We can more easily grasp the omnipotence of God or His omniscience as we learn the secrets of nature and even discover how to harness nature's power, but the concept of an omnipresent God escapes the full grasp of finite reason.

Virtually all other religions except Judaism and Islam really think of God as something impersonal, as something less than personal. If you are looking for a personal God and yet something more than a person, then, as C. S. Lewis reminded us, Christianity is the only option. It is the reality of the Trinity that explains Christianity's understanding of God as a superpersonal Deity beyond personality.

The difficulty in grasping this Christian truth results from the age-old conflict between matter and spirit, between the physical and the spiritual world. Other world religions usually focus on the spirit and reject the physical, as does Hinduism, or they affirm the physical and deny the spiritual, as does atheism. It is the Christian doctrine of the Trinity that sheds light on this challenging reality.

Mortimer Adler, the philosopher turned Christian, acknowledges that both a degree of clarity and at the same time an element of mystery will always characterize our knowledge of God. Karl Barth said that all theological constructions are inadequate to plumb the depth of God's nature, particularly the three-in-oneness of the divine Godhead.[19] And yet the doctrine of the Trinity provides the Christian with a model for dealing with the unity in diversity we see within the Godhead.

C. S. Lewis uses the reality found in the three dimensions of a cube to illustrate how God can be a person yet at the same time be beyond personality. Lewis shows that the one dimension employs only a straight line. If you use two dimensions, you can draw a figure such as a square. A square consists of four straight lines. However, if you go to three dimensions, you can construct a cube. A cube consists of six squares employing three dimensions.

After using this illustration Lewis asks, "Do you see the point?" A world of one dimension would be a world of straight lines. In a two-dimensional world you still get straight lines, but many lines make one figure. A three-dimensional world still has figures, but many figures make one solid body. In other words, as you advance to more real and more complicated levels, you don't leave behind you the things you found on the simpler levels. You still have them, but combined in new ways—in ways you couldn't imagine if you knew only the simpler levels.[20]

So it is with the nature of God's person.

THE SCRIPTURES HELP US TO KNOW GOD

In John 17:3 Jesus said: "This is life eternal, that they may know thee the only true God, and Jesus Christ, whom thou hast sent." The Scriptures are the written Word of God, testifying of Jesus, who came to reveal God (John 5:39). They reveal to us His person, His character, His will, His works, His love, all through the person of Jesus Christ.

While we cannot expect to comprehend the full nature and person and work of such an omnipotent Being, we still recognize the abundant evidence that He exists. While our faith does not rest on demonstration, yet it is based on good evidence.

A Christian perspective provides a framework in which reason and logic discover more than adequate evidence to believe in a personal God. Faith rests on "the substance of things hoped for, the *evidence* of things not seen" (Heb. 11:1).

A PERSONAL TESTIMONY OF A PERSONAL GOD

A weary Wernher von Braun walked along the desert road near the U.S. Army missile testing site at White Sands, New Mexico. World War II was over. Von Braun and his team of German rocket experts had just surrendered to the Allies. Never having wanted to use his skills for warfare, the world's greatest rocket expert hoped now to be a part of a peaceful space venture.

An old bus lumbered by and stopped at a house up ahead. Von Braun noticed "Church of the Nazarene, El Paso" written on the side. Investigating, he found that the pastor drove the old bus 50 miles every Sunday to pick up people for worship in a wooden barracks.

Sunday after Sunday Von Braun watched the bus come by the missile site. It awakened memories of his Lutheran childhood in Germany. Events during his years of scientific study and work in Germany had undercut his religious faith. Yet he knew that if human beings were to survive on earth, our only hope lay in higher values than those of science.

Aware of an aching spiritual void, he began serious Bible study. "'The truth of Christ emerged like a revelation,' he recalls. 'I realized I had been a Christian in name only.'"[21]

He moved his family to Huntsville, Alabama, where he became director of the George C. Marshall Space Flight Center. The Von Brauns joined the local Episcopal Church of the Nativity. As the space program accelerated to the point where powerful rockets, designed and built by the Von Braun team, began sending men to the moon, his personal faith grew.

Von Braun received more invitations to speak about his faith than he could handle. For example, he spoke at the Colorado governor's prayer breakfast in Denver on the subject "A Scientist's Belief in God." "The public has a deep respect for the amazing scientific advances made within our lifetime," the high-cheekboned, blond space expert said. "There is admiration for the scientific process of observation, experimentation, of testing every concept to measure its validity. But it still bothers some people that we cannot prove scientifically that God exists. Must we light a candle to see the sun?"[22]

"Many who believe in God as Creator," he added, "have difficulty accepting Him as a personal God who is interested, not only in the human race, but in the individual."

After noting that "man can know God only by His self-revelation in the person of Jesus Christ, as witnessed by Scripture," he declared, "In our search to know God . . . Jesus Christ should be the focus of our efforts, and our inspiration."[23]

Von Braun clearly confessed his faith in a personal God who revealed Himself through Jesus of Nazareth. We can know this personal God. And it is in Him alone that humanity can find the answers to life's most difficult questions. Only then will ultimate meaning and purpose become a reality.

---

[1] E. W. Lutzer, *Christ Among Other Gods*, pp. 27, 28.
[2] *Christianity Today*, Nov. 14, 1994, p. 39.
[3] *Ibid.*, p. 41.
[4] *Ibid.*
[5] *Ibid.*, p. 40.
[6] Quoted in *Time*, Dec. 28, 1992, p. 40.
[7] Wilbur Smith, "'Verdum' of Triumphant Christianity," *Christianity Today*, Aug. 28, 1961, p. 3.

[8] *Ibid.*

[9] Paul Edwards, ed., *Encyclopedia of Philosophy* (New York: Macmillan, 1967), vol. 1, p. 175.

[10] R. Zacharias, *Can Man Live Without God?* p. 17.

[11] *Ibid.,* p. 18.

[12] C. S. Lewis, *Mere Christianity* (New York: Macmillan Pub. Co., Inc., 1952), p. 30.

[13] *Ibid.*

[14] *Merriam Webster's Collegiate Dictionary,* 10th ed.

[15] *Ibid.*

[16] *Ibid.*

[17] Louise Bachelder, ed., *Abraham Lincoln: Wit and Wisdom* (Mount Vernon, N.Y.: Peter Pauper Press, 1965), p. 11.

[18] Ellen G. White, *Steps to Christ* (Washington, D.C.: Review and Herald Pub. Assn., 1908), p. 85.

[19] Quoted in David L. Mueller, *Karl Barth* (Waco, Tex.: Word, 1972), p. 68.

[20] C. S. Lewis, *Beyond Personality* (New York: Macmillan, 1945), p. 9.

[21] James C. Hefley, *How Great Christians Met Christ* (Chicago: Moody Press, 1973), p. 157.

[22] *Ibid.*

[23] *Ibid.,* p. 158.

TRICKED BY THE TRUTH OF A NOBLE LIE?

ONE BY ONE THE GENERATION THAT REFUSED TO BE BOUND BY THE POPE, AND RE-FUSED TO BE BOUND BY THE CHURCH, DECIDED IN AN ECSTASY OF FREEDOM THAT THEY WOULD NOT BE BOUND BY ANYTHING—NOT BY THE BIBLE, NOT BY CONSCIENCE, NOT BY GOD HIMSELF. FROM BELIEVING TOO MUCH THAT NEVER DID HAVE TO BE BELIEVED, THEY TOOK TO BELIEVING SO LITTLE THAT FOR COUNTLESS THOUSANDS HUMAN EXIS-TENCE AND THE WORLD ITSELF NO LONGER SEEMED TO MAKE ANY SENSE. POETS BEGAN TALKING ABOUT THE WASTELAND, WITH GHOSTLY LIVES, AS STEPHEN SPENDER PUT IT, "MOVING AMONG FRAGMENTARY RUINS WHICH HAVE LOST THEIR SIGNIFICANCE."[1]
—PAUL SCHERER

NO BOOK CONTAINS MORE TRUTHS OR IS MORE WORTHY OF CONFIDENCE THAN THE BIBLE; FOR NONE BRINGS MORE COMFORT TO THE SORROWING, MORE STRENGTH TO THE WEAK, OR MORE STIMULUS TO THE NOBLY AMBITIOUS; NONE MAKES LIFE SWEETER OR DEATH EASIER OR LESS SAD.[2]
—JUSTICE DAVID J. BREWER

Tricked into becoming a Christian by the truth of a noble lie? That is exactly what Loyd D. Rue, a professor of religion and philosophy at Lutheran College in Decorah, Iowa, believes has happened to millions of people. He argues that the teachings of the Bible are nothing more than myths and lies. However, he is quick to add that he believes these myths and lies have enabled multitudes to make some sense out of life.

These biblical myths, according to Rue, include the biblical worldview, the idea that human beings are at the center of existence, the bodily resurrection of Christ, and the Ten Commandments. In the past, Rue claims, they provided a framework for religious teachings that brought meaning and purpose to both individuals and to society at large.

However, at a recent symposium of the American Association for the Advancement of Science in Washington, Rue argued that science has so filled our heads that we can no longer swallow the traditional myths. They no longer speak to us and move us to a better life.[3]

However, without myths, Rue argues, all that we have left is nihilism, which considers life and the universe meaningless, resulting in a loss of idealism and morality, and a consequent fragmentation of society.

Rue believes that our greatest need is to create a new myth, a new noble lie, that squares with what we know scientifically. However, this "new illusion" must be "so imaginative and so compelling that it can't be resisted," so "beautiful and satisfying" that it will "deceive us, trick us, compel us beyond self-interest, beyond ego, beyond family, nation, race . . . that will get us pulling together, not just Americans, but that will make us one, and give solidarity of purpose."[4]

But Jesus assured us that the sincere seeker after God can have more certainty than that afforded by myths or even noble lies. We can find truthful and trustworthy answers to life's ultimate questions. "You shall know the truth," Jesus promised (John 17:3).

The apostle Paul assures us that the Old Testament Scriptures and the revelation of Christ in the New Testament are not myths and lies, but God speaking truth to us. He writes that "in the past God spoke to our forefathers through the prophets at many times and in various ways, but in these last days he has spoken to us by his Son" (Heb. 1:1, 2, NIV).

Through Christ, the second member of the Godhead, God reveals Himself to us in these last days. The person and work of Christ unfold a clear and trustworthy revelation of God. In Jesus we find the Word of God incarnate—God's Word in comprehensible human form, His thoughts made audible. And that revelation of Christ appears only in the written Word of God. In Christ, as revealed in Scripture, both in the Old and the New Testament, God speaks to us directly (Rom. 16:26).

THE CHRIST OF SCRIPTURE

The life and teachings of Christ speak directly to the longing of our hearts and the deepest inquiry of our minds. Christ in His preexistence, Christ in His incarnation, Christ in His life and ministry, Christ in His suffering and death, Christ in His resurrection, Christ in His priestly mediation, Christ in His coming again—all reveal to us the true and living God. These great themes provide answers to the ultimate questions of life: What and who is God? What is humanity? Where did we come from? Why are we here? What of the future? Consequently, a knowledge of Christ brings meaning and purpose to us. How then can we know Christ? The only Christ we know is the Christ of Scripture— the written Word of God. Meaning and purpose then come as we view the Scriptures as a trustworthy revelation of Christ.

Throughout Christian history believers have viewed the Bible as the supernaturally revealed Word of God and consequently fully trustworthy. Martin Luther, the primary founder of Protestantism, risked his life to defend the full inspiration and authority of Scripture. His clear and direct words express well his view of the Bible: "The Scriptures have been spoken by the Holy Ghost."[5] "In Scripture, you are reading not the word of man, but the word of the most exalted God."[6]

The apostle Peter claimed something very similar when he wrote, "You must understand that no prophecy of Scripture came about by the prophet's own interpretation. For prophecy never had its origin in the will of man, but men spoke from God as they were carried along by the Holy Spirit" (2 Peter 1:20, 21, NIV). Paul writes that "all Scripture is God-breathed" (2 Tim. 3:16, NIV). The Phillips translation says the Scriptures were "inspired by God" and the King James Version, "given by inspiration of God."

NEW THEOLOGICAL WINDS BLOWING

However, today new winds are blowing through the theological world. Some claim that the term *revelation,* as known in the past, is "unbiblical, unintelligible, and incoherent."[7] One theologian argues that "the very idea that the Bible is revealed is a claim that creates more trouble than it is worth."[8] Then he states unequivocally that the debates and discussions regarding the doctrine of revelation that have dominated theology from the 1920s to the 1960s have led into a blind alley and have resulted in complex conceptual and epistemological tangles that are difficult to understand and nearly impossible to unravel.[9]

WHAT ABOUT THE HISTORICAL-CRITICAL METHOD?

A growing number of theologians condemn the older methods of interpreting the Bible and exalt their own views above the word of God Himself. Many of these new approaches to interpreting the Bible claim the Bible is basically a human work filled with human misconceptions and errors. Consequently, they tell us that the Scriptures are as much the work of human beings as of God.

These unbiblical views of Scripture claim that inspiration touches only a kernel of truth found in the text. The Bible consists primarily of a cultural shell that we must peel away in order to discover that core of truth.

This approach holds that it is not the text's obvious meaning that is inspired, but only a principle or theological message hidden behind the Bible writer's obvious meaning that constitutes the divine revelation from God. Consequently, new methods of Bible study attempt to get beyond the obvious meaning of Scripture to discover some secret message that the scholars believe lies buried beneath the human debris of Scripture. Bible study, according to these newer methods, must not focus on the obvious, but pierce through to the meaning supposedly hidden somewhere in the text.

It appears to this student that much teaching of the Bible in theological schools has fallen into the grip of a modern form of Gnosticism, which is the belief that it is necessary to look beyond the plain sense of Scripture to a higher knowledge that lies above or behind the text. Such "Gnostic" teachers attempt to put their students in the know so that they will be privy to an esoteric knowledge that even the most intelligent and educated ordinary believers cannot get from their reading of the Scriptures.[10] It is no surprise that many evangelical theologians are adrift in the sea of modern liberalism.

What's wrong with the modern approach to biblical studies commonly referred to as the historical-critical method of interpreting the Bible? It's the built-in assumption that all writing, including Scripture, is only human in origin and nothing more! Why, some critics ask, can't God speak to me through the experience of the Bible writers rather than through what they say? "They can because we say so! We know about these things. Trust us!" the critics cry.

Would a loving God speak to us through words with no intellectually honest content, no evident meaning or purpose—just hot air that wounds and scalds the human soul? Never!

RESULTS OF THE NEW APPROACH

Using this approach, one prominent author concludes that Christ's command to wash one another's feet (John 13:14, 15) was purely a cultural practice limited to that age and locality. Consequently, foot washing does not apply to other cultures and other ages. The washing of feet was the cultural shell. The kernel of truth in it calls us to serve others by performing often dirty and menial services for them.[11]

Another writer concludes that the views of Creation in Genesis 1 do not reflect reality, but represent a mythical concept of Creation believed at the time Genesis was written. "We must recognize," he says, "that the Bible writer simply accepts the cosmology of his day, never questioning it, then uses the cosmology to convey his basic message."[12] The author of the article seeks to show that the literal week of Genesis 1 is simply a literary device for teaching only that God created. According to him, Genesis makes no attempt to give the details as to when and how God made this earth.[13]

Still another scholar employs the liberal critical methodologies as a means of proving that the resurrection of Christ was only a spiritual resurrection. Christ's physical body was not raised from the dead, he claims. But to take that position contradicts the plainest teaching of Christ regarding the future of the human race and the coming kingdom of God.

Rather than allowing the Word of God to interpret itself, this new approach denies the full inspiration of Scripture, destroys its authority, and makes the interpreter the final court that decides what is the real meaning and what is not.

When one of the professors in my doctoral program presented these new methods with their claims that the Bible contains human errors and mistakes, one student asked how the Bible could then serve as the authority needed to bring unity to the church. "The Bible is not the final authority," the professor argued.

"Where, then, is the authority needed to determine what in Scripture is fully inspired and what is not?" the student responded.

"The church gave us the Bible in the beginning; the church has rewritten it many times; therefore, the church must be the final authority," he replied.

Next the student asked, "What church, then, becomes the authority?" Immediately the professor changed the subject and turned quickly to another topic.

CHRISTIANITY AND SCIENCE ON SIMILAR GROUND?

Christians, as do scientists, utilize the tools of logic and reason in understanding God's revelation. Both theologians and scientists recognize that any view of reality rests on certain assumptions. Given those assumptions, viewing the Bible as an infallible revelation of God makes sense. Reject those assumptions, and anything goes. No system works without basic assumptions.

Although laced with its own assumptions, antitheistic science is witty and often caustic in its attacks on Christian beliefs. Many sincere individuals, not aware that all belief systems rest on certain assumptions, often play right into its hands and come to agree that faith is irrational and contrary to reason.

Also, secular science struggles with contradictions that some have always explained away with the promise "Sooner or later we'll figure out this apparent contradiction with additional scientific research." Yet these same thinkers jeer when theologians use essentially the same arguments in confronting our own contradictions and conflicts—and religious people accept it with hanging heads and red faces.

Yet we find little difference between the methodologies of the two areas of inquiry—just the consequences. Secular science begins with unprovable assumptions based upon their worldview/cultural paradigm, which leads inevitably, as history dramatically shows, to angst, despair, meaninglessness, purposelessness, pointlessness, absurdity, violence, chaos—and ultimate despair!

In a way very similar to science, biblical theological studies employ some equally unprovable assumptions based upon the Bible's worldview/cultural paradigm, which lead just as inevitably, as history also demonstrates, to existential security, meaning, purpose, direction, clarity, peace, virtue, morality—and ultimate hope and joy!

The Christian's understanding of truth begins with some absolutely glorious basic assumptions, just as secular science does, and we make no apology for them. Moreover, our assumptions start with the idea of absolute truth. They end with the belief that human beings can know those truths. Given the assumptions that a personal Creator-God brought the worlds into existence and made human beings in His own image, the Christian faith is perfectly reasonable, rational, and plausible.

To believe automatically the conclusions of antitheistic science and reject the truth claims of Christianity is nonsensical. There is really little difference in their approach, only in their conclusions.

HEURISTIC THEORIES OF KNOWLEDGE

Many of science's conclusions grow out of hypotheses resulting from laboratory research that demonstrate their correctness. However, many other conclusions drawn by science are assumptions developed from what is called "heuristic" theories of knowledge. Such theories provide knowledge based on good evidence, but which cannot be proved by factual demonstration.[14] One example is the belief that energy is conserved (does not vanish) in physical processes. Another is the theory of evolution. Both theories are assumptions or strong convictions based on observable evidence, but not facts demonstrated in a laboratory.[15]

This sort of scientific knowledge is quite similar to that undergirding the Christian worldview. We cannot always substantiate Christian faith by factual demonstration, but it nevertheless rests on ample evidence available to all.

An example that validates the authority of the Bible can be seen when we examine the argument that the Flood story in Genesis 6 and 7 derives from the Gilgamesh epic, an ancient text thought to be older than the Bible. However, the theory faces many problems. To consider just one, the Gilgamesh epic depicts the ark as a perfect cube, what the ancient Mesopotamians considered the perfect shape and the shape of the home of the gods. Can you see the implications of this fact?

A cube-shaped ship is worthless. It would sink in the first storm. But the biblical ark was eminently seaworthy, something we know because people have built other ships with virtually the same dimensions as those of the biblical ark. The battleship *Oregon*, 348 feet long and 69 feet wide, had similar size and proportions as to length and width as did the ark.[16] Obviously, the *Oregon* was a seaworthy vessel and good evidence that the biblical record and description of the ark is trustworthy.

Rather than the biblical story copying the Gilgamesh epic, it is not difficult to see the Gilgamesh epic as a corrupted copy of the true Flood story. Furthermore, archaeological research has validated many aspects of

biblical history. While we cannot reproduce historical events in a laboratory, we still find ample evidence to believe that they actually happened.

We can see, then, that the difference between the basis of
Christian beliefs and the theories of secular science virtually disap-
pears when we compare religious faith with the heuristic theories of
scientific knowledge rather than the factual conclusions of science
drawn from laboratory research.

I make no apologies, have no hesitancy, exhibit no bashfulness, in
proclaiming faith in a personal God and His revelation as rational,
reasonable, and intellectually defensible. Even though fallible human
beings wrote the Bible, it is not myth and fable! It is the infallible
Word of the living God!

CHRIST'S VIEW OF THE AUTHORITY OF SCRIPTURE

For Christians the critical factor in our view of the Scripture is the
attitude of Jesus. He is the norm for the Christian, and the way He regards the authority of Scripture is the Christian way. Jesus' view of
Scripture is determinative for the Christian.

What then does the divine record tell us about Jesus' attitude toward the Bible? While we may not fully understand the way Jesus
viewed Scripture, it is clear that in any discussion, when Jesus said "It
is written," that ended the matter.

Take, for example, the conclusion to the parable of the wicked
husbandman: "What then will the owner of the vineyard do to them?
He will come and kill those tenants and give the vineyard to others"
(Luke 20:15, 16, NIV). The Jews interjected, "May this never be." To
which Jesus replied, "Then what is the meaning of that which is written: 'the stone the builders rejected has become the capstone'?" (verses
16, 17, NIV). His answer makes sense only within the perspective that
Jesus held a high view of Scriptures and considered the Bible to be reliable and authoritative.

Another example of the fact that Jesus viewed the Scriptures as the
final authority appears in the way He handled the question of the
Sadducees regarding the woman who had seven husbands in succes-
sion. The Sadducees did not believe in the resurrection. But for Jesus
the Old Testament was decisive. He quoted Exodus 3:6, which states
that God is the God of Abraham, Isaac, and Jacob. Then He com-

mented: "He is not the God of the dead, but of the living. You are badly mistaken" (Mark 12:27, NIV). The text clearly establishes the fact that the forebears would live again in the resurrection.

Christ rejected the position of the Sadducees because it did not harmonize with Scripture. Jesus could not accept whatever did not harmonize with Scripture. And He taught that if a person rejected the Scriptures, they had no other way to learn truth. In the parable of the rich man and Lazarus, the man in hell wanted Abraham to send Lazarus to his five brothers and warn them about hell. Jesus made it clear that those who would not accept the Old Testament Scriptures as a final authority would not be convinced by miracles either. Even the witness of a person raised from the dead would not change their mind (Luke 16:19-31).

Some argue that when Jesus quoted Scripture He was simply using an argument that would carry conviction to the people of His day, granted their view of the Bible. That may have been the case in some situations, but certainly not in His quoting of Scripture in the temptation narratives, in which no one was present but Jesus and Satan. His use of Scripture under those circumstances grew out of His own convictions about the Bible. Each time Satan came to tempt Him, Jesus refuted his temptation by a quote from Scripture, used authoritatively with the introductory phrase "It is written" (Matt. 4:4, 7, 10; Luke 4:4, 8, 12).

WHAT OF THE APPARENT ERRORS IN SCRIPTURE?

Christians have never denied that one finds problems in Scripture that are difficult to explain. They include seeming contradictions and apparent errors. However, the Christian church has never in the past seen these problems as undermining the authority of the Bible as the infallible and unerring Word of God.[17]

Christ Himself affirms that the Scriptures are an inspired revelation of God. He referred often to the Old Testament, indicating that the Old Testament is a valid history of our world and of God's dealings with humanity. He spoke of Adam and Eve, the Flood, Jonah and the whale, and other people and events of the Old Testament in such a way as to show that He believed they were real people and valid historical events.

Keeping in mind the purpose of the Bible writer in writing will go a long way toward resolving many of the apparent contradictions we may find. One example is the record of Christ's temptations that Matthew and Luke give in a different order. Matthew places the second temptation on the pinnacle of the Temple, while Luke records it as being the third temptation. Both cannot be correct. This should cause no difficulty to the candid mind. The evangelists do not profess to be guided scrupulously by chronological sequence. The events are what is important, and we find no substantial difference in the description or the meaning of the three events.

While we take the problems in Scripture seriously, our faith assumptions enable us to accept the Scriptures as the fully inspired, infallible Word of God. A thoughtful spiritual person knows that in the divine as well as the human we encounter certain antinomies that mere human understanding finds at times irreconcilable and yet perfectly capable of being fused into unity by the divinely enlightened reason (1 Cor. 2:11, 14).

While we might spend valuable time in trying to resolve the difficult problems in Scripture in order to prove the Bible authoritative, it is more consistent to regard the Scriptures as reliable because that was the view of Christ and the apostles. Leon Morris points out that "it is this, and not our ability to explain the difficulties, that is the justification for our holding the Bible to be God's authoritative revelation."[18]

WHY DO WE STUDY THE BIBLE?

While we study the Bible to discover the truth about God, human beings, our world, evil, the future, etc., our primary purpose in reading Scripture must always be to find God Himself. While we reject the idea that the essence of revelation is encounter, we believe that encounter is important. The Bible is but the means to the end of bringing us into relationship with God. It is the means whereby we realize our lost state and find salvation in Jesus Christ. We cannot overemphasize this fact.

The great revelations of Scripture seek to lead us to know God and desire a relationship with Him. Only through faith in Christ is this possible. Jesus made this point when He said, "Unless you eat the flesh of the Son of Man and drink his blood, you have no life in you" (John 6:53, NIV). Spiritual understanding and life grow out of a focused relationship with Christ—the Christ of Scripture. And this relationship gives meaning to life.

Viewing Scripture as a revelation of God in Christ enables us to unveil the mystery of God and unscramble the puzzle of life. To know God in Christ is to discover not only the meaning of life but also to find life itself. It is the love of God seen in Christ that changes us and restores in us the image of God.

By beholding God's love, by dwelling upon it, we become partakers of His nature. What food is to the body, Christ must be to the soul. Food cannot benefit us unless we eat it, unless it becomes a part of our being. So Christ is of no value if we do not know Him as a personal Saviour. And it is through the Scriptures that we come to know Christ.

"The life of Christ that gives life to the world is in His Word. It was by His word that Jesus healed disease and cast out demons; by His word He stilled the sea, and raised the dead. . . . The whole Bible is a manifestation of Christ, and the Saviour desired to fix the faith of His followers on the Word. When His visible presence should be withdrawn, the Word must be their source of power. . . . As our physical life is sustained by food, so our spiritual life is sustained by the Word of God"[19]

Dwelling upon the Word of God engraves in our memory the very mind of Christ. He then lives within us, guiding and sustaining us. We come to know Christ's thoughts, God's thoughts. Faith grows, hope springs anew, and spiritual healing and life result.

Then we will know that the Bible is not a myth or even a noble lie. It is the living Word of God that authenticates itself by answering life's ultimate questions, thereby bringing humanity the greatest meaning and purpose a person can possibly know.

---

[1] Paul Scherer, in R. Zacharias, *Can Man Live Without God?* p. xv.

[2] David J. Brewer, in Howard Hyde Russell, *A Lawyer's Examination of the Bible* (Westerville, Ohio: Bible Bond Inc., 1935), p. 14.

[3] Chattanooga *News-Free Press,* July 20, 1991.

[4] *Ibid.*

[5] *Martin Luther's Works,* St. Louis edition, Vol. ix, p. 1890.

[6] *Ibid.,* p. 1818.

[7] Ronald F. Thiemann, *Revelation and Theology: The Gospel as Narrative Promise* (Notre Dame, Ind.: Notre Dame Press, 1985), p. 1.

[8] *Ibid.*

[9] *Ibid.*

[10] Richard John Newhouse, in *First Things,* June/July 1994, p. 72.

[11] John R. W. Stott, *Culture and the Bible* (Downers Grove, Ill.: InterVarsity Press, 1979), p. 29.

[12] *Spectrum* 13, No. 2: 57.

[13] *Ibid.*

[14] Robert E. D. Clark, *Science and Christianity* (Mountain View, Calif.: Pacific Press Pub. Assn., 1972), p. 70.

[15] *Ibid.*

[16] Alfred M. Rehwinkel, *The Flood in the Light of the Bible, Geology, and Archaeology* (St. Louis: Concordia Publishing House, 1951), p. 59.

[17] Kenneth Kantzer, "Why I Still Believe the Bible Is True," *Christianity Today,* Oct. 7, 1988, p. 22.

[18] Leon Morris, *I Believe in Revelation* (Grand Rapids: William B. Eerdmans Pub. Co., 1976), p. 140.

[19] Ellen G. White, *The Desire of Ages* (Mountain View, Calif.: Pacific Press Pub. Assn., 1898), p. 390.

CHAPTER 6

THE GOD-MAN

WHY DOES MAN FEEL SO SAD IN THE TWENTIETH CENTURY? WHY DOES MAN FEEL SO SAD IN THE VERY AGE WHEN, MORE THAN IN ANY OTHER AGE, HE HAS SUCCEEDED IN SATISFYING HIS NEEDS AND MAKING THE WORLD OVER FOR HIS OWN USE?[1]
—WALTER PERCY

DEEP IN MAN IS FOUND AN AWARENESS THAT THE MATERIAL WORLD AND TEMPORAL LIFE CANNOT SATISFY HIS LONGING FOR DIVINE RELATIONSHIP AND AN IDENTITY WITH ETERNAL REALITIES. IF WE DEFINE RELIGION AS "THE RECOGNITION OF MAN'S RELATION TO A DIVINE OR SUPERHUMAN POWER TO WHOM OBEDIENCE AND REVERENCE ARE DUE," WE WILL FIND THAT RELIGION IS A NATURAL CONDITION OF LIFE. THE SENSE OF THE TRANSCENDENT IS AT THE HEART OF TRUE HUMANNESS.[2]
—V. NORSKOV OLSEN

Arthur Schopenhauer, the great German philosopher of pessimism, spent his life reading, thinking, writing, and lecturing about the challenging questions about the mysteries of the universe and particularly about humanity. As Schopenhauer grew older, he loved to do his thinking as he walked in the city park of Berlin. Often he could be seen walking or sitting with uncombed hair and wrinkled clothes. Once while Schopenhauer was sitting on a park bench, eyes closed in deep thought, a policeman, seeing him in his unkempt dress and apparently sleeping, mistook him for a tramp. Shaking him, the officer demanded, "Who are you and what are you doing here?"

Schopenhauer, still pondering the unintelligibility of the universe and the dark mystery of the human race, answered, "I wish to God I knew!"

For millions of moderns, Schopenhauer's words paint a plaintive picture all too close to reality. Few have satisfying or plausible answers to life's urgent questions. Millions do not know where they came from, who they are, why they are in this world, or what their future holds.

SEEKING ANSWERS

Philosophy, science, medicine, theology, sociology, history—all concern themselves with the bottom-line questions of life. The Enlightenment claimed that there were answers and that one could discover them by logic and reason alone. However, modern philosophy blatantly argues that there are no concrete answers, no fixed truth. M. Scott Peck, a well-known psychiatrist-writer, affirms this view and argues that we can only speculate, theorize, or postulate hypotheses about humanity and its world.[3]

Bertrand Russell underscored this sense of meaninglessness in a more graphic and despairing way when he wrote: "Man is the product of causes which had no provision of the end they were achieving; that his origin, his growth, his hopes and his fears, his loves and his beliefs, are but the outcome of accidental collocations of atoms; that no fire, no heroism, no intensity of thought and feeling can preserve an individual life beyond the grave. That all the labors of the ages, all the devotion, all the inspiration, all the noonday brightness of human genius are destined to extinction in the vast death of the solar system, that the whole temple of man's achievement must inevitably be buried beneath the debris of a universe in ruins."[4]

If there are no answers, then Jean-Paul Sartre, the French existentialist, was right when he said a human being is simply "a bubble of consciousness in an ocean of nothingness, bobbing around until the bubble pops." Could it be that human beings are nothing more than bobbing bubbles, fleeting sparks, or the fiery tail of a shooting star, visible only for a moment, then disappearing forever?

The answer is an unequivocal no! A human being is much more. There are answers, answers that bring meaning and purpose.

WHERE HUMANITY CAME FROM

The pivotal Christian assumption holds that a personal God created human beings. A reasonable assumption? we ask. Much more reasonable than an accident of evolution. The probability that human beings are a result of biological evolution is one in 100 billion. What thinking person would bet on those odds?

John Stuart Mill spoke to the logic of special creation when he said: "Among the facts of the universe to be accounted for, it may be said, is mind; and it is self-evident that nothing can have produced mind, but mind."[5] The mind that he refers to is nothing more than the mind of God. That Mind is the Creator-God. Paul looked into this reality when he wrote: "For from him and through him and to him are all things" (Rom. 11:36, NIV). A. M. Fairbairn, of Oxford, said: "The first and last, the highest and the surest thing in nature is the thought which explains nature, but which nature cannot explain."[6]

George Washington affirmed this seminal point when he stated: "It is impossible to reason without arriving at a supreme Being." Without the concept of God we are left with meaninglessness. Chance means chaos, while design means order. If there is a God, a designer, then there is a design and purpose to everything that we see. The ancient saying *Nihil ex nihil fit* ("Nothing comes from nothing") expresses this truth well.

The principle of cause and effect dictates every conclusion even in the area of science. There must be an absolute and ultimate causality. God is that first cause, the prime mover of every living thing.

Thus we can unravel the dark mystery of the human race only as we begin with God. John Calvin, the famous Reformer, drives this point home. "It is evident that man never attains the true self-knowledge until he has previously contemplated the face of God and comes down after such contemplation to look into himself."[7]

WHAT OR WHO IS THE HUMAN RACE?

Being created in the divine image, humanity is itself an image of God. We bear a godlikeness. V. Norskov Olsen sees two analogies by which we may compare human beings to God.[8]

A. That of an image of a king stamped on a coin. This analogy sees human beings as having a resemblance to God, a resemblance that helps us to begin to define the nature of humanity. However, if we deny or do not understand this God-given resemblance, then man is no longer man in the strictest sense of the word. Consequently, human beings lose their sense of identity and any sense of meaning and purpose.

B. Human beings, created in the image of God, are similar to a reflection of a person in a mirror. A mirror can reflect an image only if an object is in front of it. So human beings exist only in relationship to God. If anything disrupts the relationship, then human identity also vanishes. That is why Paul acknowledges human beings as the offspring of God (Acts 17:28). If human beings begin with God, then life's greatest questions are answered and we find meaning, purpose, and hope. And this is why John Calvin said that true self-knowledge comes only as we believe that we are the children of God.

God alone made human beings on this earth in His image. Consequently, we possess a godlike intelligence, including a consciousness pervaded by reason. We are endowed with a capacity for knowledge, for love, for an appreciation of moral values, and with the gift of free decision that empowers us to respond to revealed values and particularly to God.

We accomplish this by intentional relationships that allow us to freely and consciously participate in the world around us. Who has not stood on the ocean's shore watching the breakers rise higher and higher until they finally crash against the shore, then explode into a thousand rivulets of sparkling light? A person's emotions and mind have to be numb not to participate consciously in such a wondrous reality.

Yet to participate consciously in God's existence far exceeds all other experiences, bringing with it the greatest sense of being, of permanence, of meaning and purpose, that we can possibly ever know. To know God, to form concepts of Him, to enter into a conscious relationship with Him, to contemplate Him, as it were, eye-to-eye and face-to-face, is the greatest possible purpose in life.

A consciousness of the mystery of God first awakened in my mind as a 6-year-old boy. It took place in a simple Methodist church in southeastern Oklahoma. Great old hymns of praise bracketed a sermon on God's greatness that concluded with prayer in which the entire congregation knelt beside their pews. While I did not have enough knowledge to apprehend God's reality intellectually, I sensed for the first time the awesome presence of the divine Being referred to in the preaching and the hymns.

However, it was not until I was 23 years of age that I went through what we often refer to as conversion, in which I intellectually apprehended the reality of God, sensed His love for me, and consciously sought His presence, His acceptance, and His transforming power in my life. God responded that night in a way that words cannot fully explain. For a brief few moments, which seemed like an eternity, I entered into being with God and became one with Him who inhabits eternity. It was a magic moment, a transforming one. That place became a sacred place, a place of worship, the secret place of the Most High. I felt like Jacob when he said, "Surely the Lord is in this place; and I did not know it" (Gen. 28:16, RSV).

That brief encounter with the God of Abraham, Isaac, and Jacob birthed the most transformational experience of my life. It forever changed my life and its direction, an encounter that now comes to me often when alone with God in study and prayer, an enlightenment of the highest order that I cannot keep secret. It must be shared. And the sharing of the spiritual realities that make known the true and living God, revealed in the life and teaching of Jesus, brings to me the greatest meaning and purpose I could ever wish to know.

GOD'S PURPOSE IN CREATING HUMANITY

Being created in the image of God makes us creative beings. Through our investigative spirit and creative or inventive mind, we reveal and discover our kinship to God and the reason for our existence. It is wonderfully rewarding to ponder the fact of our creation in the divine image. Couple that with the first words of Genesis, "God created," which constitute the defining statement of God's nature, and we begin to grasp the essence of our purpose in life.

Ellen White expresses this transcendent truth beautifully when she writes: "Human beings were a new and distinct order. They were made 'in the image of God.' . . . God created man a superior being; he alone is formed in the image of God, and is capable of partaking of the divine nature, of cooperating with his Creator in executing His plans."[9]

The central characteristic common to both God and human beings is apparently the desire and ability to make things. However, it is only as we see ourselves as created in the image of God that we awaken to an awareness of our creative possibilities. While we will always be dependent upon God, we have the possibility of a constant and more full unfolding of His creative powers, ever more fully realizing the creative purposes for which we were made. For late-twentieth-century men and women that means many things. But all of those things focus on the work of restoring in the human race God's image and this planet to its Edenic beauty and perfection. "Higher than the highest human thought can reach is God's ideal for His children. Godliness—god-likeness—is the goal to be reached."[10]

REALIZING OUR DESTINY

The fact of our creation teaches us that we are dependent beings. Our problem is that we have lost our sense of creatureliness. This confusion first overtook the human race when it rejected its dependence in Eden. The first human beings chose to break their relationship with their Creator and thus lost their sense of dependence. Our only other option is to believe that we are God ourselves.

That is exactly what M. Scott Peck and millions of other moderns postulate. Scott embraces an evolutionary worldview and consequently holds a concept of God that is muddled at best and pantheistic at worst. A heretical view of humanity follows hard on the heals of such a confused worldview. "God," Scott writes, "wants us to become Himself or Herself or Itself. We are growing toward Godhood. God is the goal of evolution."[11]

Millions have come to believe these New Age concepts and consequently are working at cross-purposes with God. The devastating results are the same today as always. One sincere person who had gotten involved with New Age teaching burned this reality into my mind. "I would give anything if I had never gotten involved. It scrambled my mind, broke up my family, and cost me my career."

Believing that we are God when we are not explains our present dilemma. The Bible calls this self-centeredness sin. Whether a person believes the story of Adam and Eve literally or metaphorically, one cannot deny the pregnant truth it conveys. When people turn away from God, confusion, fear, anxiety, suffering, and chaos quickly follow.

Modern life confronts us with a striking paradox. On the one hand, we are tempted to conceive of human beings as being unlimited in their evolution, capable of dominating nature and of changing the world into a terrestrial paradise or even possibly prolonging human life indefinitely. On the other hand, when we deny our spiritual nature, we discover that we lose our capacity for objective knowledge plus our free will that enables us to cooperate with God in our restoration. Thus we come to view life only as a result of physiological and psychological processes and limit love and happiness to the outworking of chemistry.

Apart from our sense of relationship to God, our creatureliness, we are left with only ourselves and the laws of nature to assure our future and destiny. History chronicles the horrific evils of this view of an independent humanity. The indescribable suffering and death of more than 45 million individuals resulted from Nazi Germany's efforts to create a godless utopia.

Conversely, acknowledging our dependence upon God and entering into a conscious relationship with Him enable us to reach the destiny for which He made us. Moses, possibly the greatest historical character that ever lived, achieved all that he did only in the consciousness of God's presence and power in his life. When challenged to lead a newly freed nation a thousand miles across wilderness and desert, Moses agreed to do so with one condition: that God would go with him. "If thy presence go not with me, carry us not up hence" (Ex. 33:15). And what was God's promise? "My presence shall go with thee, and I will give thee rest" (verse 14). Knowing that God's presence would accompany him, Moses was able to lead the motley crowd of Jewish slaves to a new country, molding them into a disciplined and powerful nation.

THE CALL TO VALUES

The fact of human creatureliness is a call to values that play a crucial role in realizing our destiny. And yet these values—reverence, obedience, self-discipline, and gratitude—are alien to us. We resist abandoning ourselves to any values or authority outside of ourselves. On the contrary, everything becomes a means for our arbitrary pleasure and satisfaction. Freedom, sexuality, education, material things—we use them all to satisfy self. Then we witness in the daily newspaper the violent and bloody results of denying these values.

Modern humanity's flagrant flaunting of values is worse than that of the old paganism. At least the pagans had a sense of dependence upon a higher power and being to whom they must submit themselves. Contemporary humanity rejects every authority, seeing itself as the

71

center of existence and dependent on nothing. Consequently, we have nothing external to guide or help us. We have jettisoned all sense of morality, all sense of right and wrong. It is interesting to note that in the long run we cannot remain inconsistent to what we believe. That which we profess in theory shapes not only our attitudes, but the way we live.

That is why a person can believe a lie and still be damned. While the lie may give us a sense of freedom and progress toward some higher life, after a certain time the errors in our understanding turn life sour. An attitude of indifference and disrespect for truth, for reality, leads us counter to reality. Left to ourselves, we grope in the darkness toward our own destruction. No wonder we moderns find ourselves menaced by a mysterious rupture and disharmony. Wherever I travel, speaking about meaning and purpose, many, particularly disillusioned young people, tell me they feel disconnected, unplugged, powerless, and alone in life. Todd, a handsome yet confused young man, told me that he constantly thought about suicide, but didn't have the courage to kill himself.

Modern philosophies have cut us loose from objective reality, from God, from an understanding of our creatureliness. Few see a need for any external objective principles to guide them. One shudders at our rebellion against the sense of absolute truth. Many ridicule objective truth as myth and legend, anachronisms consigned to the junk heaps of yesteryear. Modern satanism is exhibit A.

According to Anton La Vey, founder of the Church of Satan, satanism views human beings as potentially divine. The satanist realizes, La Vey claims, "that man, and the actions and reaction of the universe, is responsible for everything."[12]

Satanism regards the Bible as a most insidious document and claims that there is nothing inherently sacred about moral codes.

Rejecting the self-sacrificing attitude of Christianity, the satanic bible demands of the Christian: "I request reasons for your golden rule and ask the why and wherefore of your ten commands. . . . No hoary falsehood shall be a truth to me, no stifling dogma shall encramp my pen. . . . I gaze into the glassy eyes of your fearsome Jehovah, and pluck him by the beard; I uplift a broad-axe, and split open his worm-eaten skull."[13]

Irregardless of what satanism claims, a meaningful and productive life is one framed by obligations. A life pervaded by the consciousness that every good possession and authentic value calls for a willing and grateful response. We accept the gift of God with thanksgiving, realizing that obligations are a necessary and valuable part of any true gift. The Christian accepts the obligation to appreciate the gifts God offers us, and commits himself or herself to protect them and to make sacrifices for their preservation.

A RELATIONSHIP WITH CHRIST

Finally, only in Christ can we acquire the genuine life that God offered in creating us. We must be reborn in Christ. Only in a dynamic relationship with Him can we realize our purpose in this life and our destiny in the life to come.

John explained this when he said, "He that hath the Son hath life; and he that hath not the Son of God hath not life" (1 John 5:12). Being dependent beings, we have life only in relationship to God in Christ. This is why Christ said that if we would abide in Him, we would bring forth much fruit (John 15).

Only as we renew and strengthen our creatureliness through a conscious relationship with Christ can we realize the possibility of a full unfolding of our personality and of our godlikeness. And to do that requires an understanding that our existence, our happiness, our growth, and our development are based not on a sovereign display of our arbitrary moods or our self-will, but upon a free cooperation with the natural and supernatural gifts of God in our lives. It depends upon a great dialogue with a reality independent of ourselves, upon transcending the realm of our own limited being, upon participating in God's infinite plentitude.

The truly human life, the realization of God's purpose for us, means that we accept our absolute dependence upon God. It is a life with all its natural insecurities, risks, and sacrifices common to Christians throughout history. Consequently, the true searcher relies upon God's providence, not on his or her own forces or on any automatic human progress.

A life filled with meaning and purpose always remains a gift from God. And realizing this gift enables us to see that life can be far more than a bubble of consciousness in an ocean of nothingness, bobbing around until the bubble bursts. We are truly in the image of God when we know where we came from, why we are here, and where we are going. We experience this certainty because our lives are pervaded by the consciousness that we came from God and in Him we can find real meaning and true purpose.

---

[1] Quoted in David F. Wells, *No Place for Truth* (Grand Rapids: William B. Eerdmans Pub. Co., 1993), p. 53.

[2] V. Norskov Olsen, *Man, the Image of God* (Washington, D.C.: Review and Herald Pub. Assn., 1988), p. 85.

[3] M. Scott Peck, *The Road Less Traveled* (New York: Simon and Schuster, 1978), p. 269.

[4] "A Free Man's Worship," in Robert Engner and Lester E. Denonn, eds., *The Writings of Bertrand Russell—1903-1959* (New York: Simon and Schuster, 1961), p. 67.

[5] John Stuart Mill, *Three Essays on Religion* (New York: Henry Holt and Co., 1874), p. 150.

[6] Burton Fairbairn, *Philosophy of Christian Religion* (New York: Macmillan Co., 1954).

[7] John Calvin, *Institutes of the Christian Religion* (Philadelphia: Westminster, 1960), book 1, vol. 20, p. 37.

[8] Olsen, pp. 28ff.

[9] Ellen G. White, *Sons and Daughters of God* (Washington, D.C.: Review and Herald Pub. Assn., 1955), p. 7.

[10] ———, *Education* (Mountain View, Calif.: Pacific Press Pub. Assn., 1903), p. 18.

[11] Peck.

[12] Anton Szansor La Vey, *The Satanic Bible* (New York: Avon Books, 1969), p. 17.

[13] *Ibid.,* p. 30.

THE PROBLEM OF EVIL

---◆---

THE PROBLEM OF EXPLAINING EVIL, WHICH OCCURS AS EARLY AS THE PHILOS-
OPHY OF PLATO (C. 427-347 B.C.), TAKES ON AN ESPECIALLY PARADOXICAL FORM
IN CHRISTIANITY BECAUSE THE LATTER AFFIRMS AT ONE AND THE SAME TIME THAT
THE CREATION IS GOOD AND THAT GOD IS ESPECIALLY REVEALED IN AN EVIL EVENT,
THE CRUCIFIXION.[1]

—VAN A. HARVEY

Former president Ronald Reagan called the now-defunct Soviet Union the "evil empire." Even a casual study of the history of Communism appears to justify this title. Stalin idealized torture and murder as a legitimate means of governing.

In 1991 the military leadership of Soviet Russia sponsored a new and official history of the "great patriotic war" against Nazi Germany. The Communist Party asked General Dmitre Antonovich Volkogonov to write the first volume. He provided conclusive documentary evidence that Stalin, using blue and red pencils, personally ordered the deaths of thousands of his own compatriots in the same offhand attitude as a man ordering a drink at a bar.[2]

How deeply Volkogonov's days in the archives moved him can be seen in the following quote:

"I remember coming home after reading through the day of December 12, 1938. He [Stalin] signed thirty lists of death sentences that day, altogether about five thousand people, including many he knew personally, his friends. This was before their trials, of course. This was no surprise. This is not what shook me. But it turned out that, having signed these documents, he went to his personal theater very late that night and watched two movies, including *Happy Guys,* a popular comedy of the time. . . . Then I understood why my father was shot, why my mother died in exile, why millions of people died."[3]

In the light of such discoveries, how could anyone deny the reality of evil? However, Harold Kushner, a well-known author, believes that what we call evil is only a transitory by-product of life. Subscribing to an evolutionary worldview, Kushner believes that the universe is moving toward equilibrium, yielding to the rule of order. He argues that the evil we experience, such as suffering and disease, is the result of retained or inherited weaknesses from those earlier years of chaos.[4]

Most who hold confused views of the nature of evil and its causes do so because of a compromised view of Scripture. This is certainly true of Kushner. He regards the Bible as a human work reflecting the same evolutionary development that he believes took place in human evolution. Consequently, what the Bible teaches he often sees as nothing more than myth and fable.[5]

Without faith in Scripture as fully the Word of God, Kushner finds himself forced to respond to the question as to why chromosomes become defective: "I have no satisfying answers. The best answer I know is the reminder that man today is only the latest stage in a long slow evolutionary process. . . . As life evolved from the simpler to the more complex, we retained and inherited some of the weaknesses of those earlier forms."[6]

His compromised view of a God restricted and governed by the laws of nature is clearly evident: "I believe in God. But I do not believe the same things about Him that I did years ago when I was a theological student. I recognize His limitations. He is limited in what He can do by the laws of nature and by the evolution of human nature."[7]

Considering children born with defective hearts that would keep them from enjoying life or making much of a contribution to the world, he concludes that we could solve the problem if we let the "sickly children die at birth, worked less diligently to help them survive childhood illnesses and hazards, permitted only the healthiest specimens to marry and have children, and forbade others to know those satisfactions."[8]

A confused view of the forces of evil usually accompanies a distorted understanding of God and humanity. Kushner makes God little better than a human being and human beings little less than God. The results are frightening indeed. Kushner would have us play God.

If we followed his suggestion to allow only the strong to live, who would decide who are the weak and who are the strong, who should die and who should live?

Coming to a clear and correct understanding of evil plays a critical role in assuring the well-being of all.

To many the origin of sin and the reason for its existence are a source of great perplexity. They see suffering and death, and ask, "If God is omnipotent and wholly benevolent, how can all this evil exist?" Especially is this true of someone experiencing the loss of a loved one. The questions rise: "Why did God allow this evil to happen to me?" "Can I continue to worship a God who does not remove the evil that seeks to destroy my happiness and security?" My father gave this same reason for not believing in God. Born a chronic asthmatic, he suffered all his life, dying at the young age of 45. From childhood he had to sleep sitting up in bed. To lie down was to suffocate. "No God would allow me to suffer the way I do!" he argued.

THE CHRISTIAN VIEW OF EVIL

According to the Bible, evil is the consequence of immoral behavior. At first God placed human beings in an idyllic garden where they lived in a happy relationship with their Creator and nature. They had the possibility of eternal life. However, the day they committed moral evil by disobeying God, they found themselves filled with guilt and shame, confusion, and fear. While God forgave them, He had to banish them from the garden and consign them to a life of sorrow and labor.

Christians believe evil is morally reprehensible or sinful. Evil then is sin. It arises from the actual misconduct or wrongdoing of God's creatures. The Old Testament tells us that evil resulted from the first man's sin, and that sin is the transgression of God's moral law. The New Testament agrees with the Old and tells us that the "wrath of God" opposes all unrighteousness (Rom. 1:18) and that "the wages of sin is death" (Rom. 6:23).

Research proves what is clearly evident. Faith in God, a life in harmony with Judeo-Christian values, guarantees a longer and more satisfying life than that offered by any other belief system.[9]

Some would have us believe that death is a friend rather than an enemy, that it is a natural part of life as it evolves upward toward perfection. That concept arises out of a nonbiblical worldview and makes God responsible for evil. Who could love and trust a God who uses evil to bring about good, suffering and death to bring about life? But the Christian sees a world gone bad by its own choice.

The Scriptures reveal that the willful breaking of God's moral law caused evil.

This takes us all the way back to the origin of evil found in the immoral behavior of one of God's brightest created beings. The prophet Isaiah reveals his name as Lucifer, a brilliant and powerful angel who rejected the moral laws of God's government and chose to experiment with different laws that he claimed would bring greater happiness and well-being to the universe (Isa. 14:12).

The Christian understands evil in the light of Lucifer's rebellion against God's government thousands of years ago in heaven (Isa. 14:12-14; Eze. 28:13-18; Rev. 12:7-9). After the creation of our world, Satan, as he was later called, made it his headquarters for his rebellion.

The conflict between God and Satan clearly illustrates the rightness of God's moral law. Lucifer, rather than exalt God and others, chose to put himself first, usurping the authority and place of God. And he would willingly use force to hurt and destroy anybody, even God, should He get in his way.

An angel trying to be God—the creature wanting to be Creator. Could this be the ground in which the seeds of all evil took root? Evil then resulted directly from the violation of the moral law by Lucifer and the angels who joined with him in warring against God's government.

These evil spirits or fallen angels not only visit this earth but also have inflicted evil on all who live here (Mark 9:20; Luke 13:10-16). Scripture attributes Job's sufferings to Satan (Job 1:6-19). Also, people in Jesus' day were said to be oppressed and afflicted with disease from the devil (Matt. 17:14-21).

Why Lucifer chose to reject that law and act independently of God will always be a mystery. We can give no explanation for the origin of evil. To find any reason or to give excuse for it would be to justify it. Yet we can understand enough concerning both the origin and the nature of evil to show its insidious nature and to prove the love and justice of God in allowing evil to exist.

Love the Basis of Moral Law

God's moral law calls for a radically different attitude than the proud and arrogant posture taken by Lucifer. Self-sacrificing service and self-forgetting love comprise the law of heaven. The first four commandments tell us how to love God, while the final six tell us how to love our fellow human beings. However, we can best grasp the loving service the law requires in Christ's willingness to take the form of a servant, to live a life of loving service to sinful men and women.

In the Garden of Eden we see our first parents—Adam and Eve—deceived by the serpent acting as a medium for Lucifer. Consequently, evil suddenly smashes into our world, robbing us of joy and life, bringing sorrow, suffering, and death. Paul reveals the origin of evil in this world when he writes that "by one man sin entered into the world, and death by sin; and so death passed upon all men, for that all have sinned" (Rom. 5:12). Evil, then, is in our blood, our genes.

Could God Prevent Evil?

Some argue that surely an omnipotent God could have prevented evil. But for God to do so would have created two very difficult problems. First, if God were to block all evil acts from occurring, He would have to interfere with the full exercise of our free choice, which would result in the loss of freedom. In a world of constant divine intervention and control over evil actions, all moral learning would cease. Human beings would never learn the evil consequences of bad choices.

A few years ago, while wrestling with a friend, I injured a nerve center in my left shoulder. Intense throbbing pain kept me awake at night. I appealed to the doctor for drugs to kill the pain. "I don't recommend it," he replied. "You will not learn anything from this problem if you kill the pain with drugs." I'm not sure what were all the lessons he thought I could learn, but his point was clear.

Why did God not destroy Satan in the beginning? Once evil entered the universe it became necessary for all to see its true nature. If God had wiped out Lucifer, angels and human beings would have ever after served God out of fear rather than out of love. God desires only the service of love. To enable us to see His love and to choose of our own free will to serve Him, God has allowed evil to exist. When all shall see that God is love and that His way is the best, then God will end all evil.

CHRISTIANITY BEST EXPLAINS EVIL

It seems evident from our study that Christianity does provide the most satisfactory answers to the problem of evil in our world. The more we come to know about the true nature of reality, with its inherent evil and evil results, we discover that the view of good and evil portrayed in Scripture and Christianity best describes the nature of reality as we actually observe it.

The Christian position holds that God created humanity in His image and placed them on earth with the power of free choice. Through their willful free choice, human beings brought evil into the world. Our sense of right and wrong testifies to the reality of a moral structure within the universe, and our bent to evil testifies to the sinfulness of that moral nature within humanity.[10]

ASSURANCE OF A BETTER WORLD IN THE FUTURE

Since there is an all-powerful God who can ultimately defeat evil without destroying free choice, we have assurance that He will eradicate evil in the future.

Christianity holds more than just the ultimate hope of the eventual destruction of evil, however. It also provides understanding, strength, and comfort to sustain us in the suffering we all experience in the meantime.

Historic Christianity teaches that God desires to restore humanity to a vital and personal relationship with Himself. This is accomplished through faith in Christ and through the substitutionary death of Christ. It is in relationship with Him that we are able to endure the evil we experience.

It was the loss of this relationship with His heavenly Father that broke Jesus' heart and wrung from His lips that anguished cry "My God, my God, why hast thou forsaken me?" (Matt. 27:46).

Christianity as well provides the only solution to evil in the hearts of human beings and in the world and universe as a whole. While sin is the breaking of the moral law, which results in evil, Christ's death on the cross provides forgiveness for any violation of God's law. Beyond that, Christianity provides power to overcome sin in what the Bible calls conversion, or the new birth. The Holy Spirit changes the human heart and sets a person's feet on a pathway that leads to conformity to God's moral law, which in turn results in harmony with God.

THE PROBLEM OF EVIL

FROM CRIMINAL TO CHRISTIAN

The life of Harry Orchard, a notorious criminal early in the twentieth century, testifies beautifully to this reality. Gambling, cheating, and stealing became a way of life for him. After he hired himself out to the labor unions, he added violence to his crimes. He dragged men from their homes, murdering them before their families.

The low point of Orchard's career of crime came when he led a lawless gang in dynamiting the Bunker Hill and Sullivan Concentrating Mill in Kellogg, Idaho, a company that refused to bend to union demands. The blast destroyed the mill, killing several employees. Frank Stunenberg, governor of Idaho, determined to bring Orchard to justice. Orchard took his wrath out on the governor. Building a small bomb, he attached it to the gate of the governor's home and waited. When the governor opened the gate, the bomb exploded, killing him instantly. The police quickly captured Orchard. The courts found him guilty and sentenced him to life in prison.

Mrs. Stunenberg, the murdered governor's wife and a devout Christian, forgave Harry Orchard and took him a little book to read, entitled *Steps to Christ*, by Ellen G. White. Finding Christ, Orchard experienced a change of heart. Throughout his long years of incarceration he exemplified the Christian life. The following statement testifies to the power of Christ to take the evil out of a person's life and give meaning and purpose even to imprisonment:

"I well remember the day that I walked into this penitentiary. As the jailer turned the key in my cell, I felt instinctively that I would never be a free man again. That was more than four decades ago. I am still incarcerated within this prison. But in spite of these years of confinement, I have a freedom of soul that I never once knew in the days when I was physically free. Stone walls and metal bars have held my body captive, but my soul has long been freed."[11]

SIN NO MORE

Finally, Christianity provides the assurance that one day evil will be annihilated from the universe, and that those who accept God's provision will receive eternal life in a perfect world. The universe will have no more evil empires. No more Stalins or Hitlers, no more mass killings or death camps. And the Word of God assures us that evil will not arise a second time (Rev. 21:1-3; Nahum 1:9).

---

[1] Van A. Harvey, *A Handbook of Theological Terms* (New York: Macmillan, 1964), p. 236.

[2] D. Remnick, *Lenin's Tomb*, p. 406.

[3] *Ibid.*

[4] Harold S. Kushner, *When Bad Things Happen to Good People* (New York: Avon, 1981), p. 66.

[5] *Ibid.*, pp. 32, 41, 52.

[6] *Ibid.*, p. 66.

[7] *Ibid.*, p. 134.

[8] *Ibid.*, p. 66.

[9] *Current Thoughts and Trends* 11, No. 5 (May 1995): 4.

[10] Norman L. Geisler, *The Roots of Evil* (Grand Rapids: Zondervan, 1978).

[11] Quoted in Bruce Johnston's written sermon "The Dynamite Killer."

A KETTLE OF BOILING FROGS

WE MUST INSIST ON THE RIDICULOUS INCONSISTENCY OF ALL THOSE WHO PRO-
FESS A DENIAL OF OBJECTIVE TRUTH AND SIMULTANEOUSLY ARROGATE OBJECTIVE
TRUTH TO THEIR THEORY. NOTHING CAN BE MORE FATAL TO A THEORY THAN TO DENY
IN ITS CONTENT WHAT IT NECESSARILY PRESUPPOSES IN THE VERY ACT OF AFFIRMING.
WE MUST NOT CEASE UNMASKING THE INEVITABLE, FLAGRANT CONTRADICTION, THAT
IS NECESSARILY INVOLVED IN EVERY ATTEMPT TO DENY OBJECTIVE TRUTH AND THE
POSSIBILITY OF ITS KNOWLEDGE.[1]

—DIETRICH VON HILDEBRAND

A SERIOUS CASUALTY OF OUR TIME THAT DEFIES COMPREHENSION IS THE DEATH
OF TRUTH. BY DENYING ABSOLUTES AND ERADICATING ALL POINTS OF REFERENCE BY
WHICH WE TEST VERACITY, OUR CIVILIZATION HAS ENTERED TERRA INCOGNITA ON
MATTERS OF THE GREATEST IMPORTANCE EVEN FOR SURVIVAL. SKEPTICISM AND CYN-
ICISM HAVE BECOME THE HALLMARKS OF SOPHISTICATION. AT LEAST, SUCH IS THE
POSTURE TAKEN BY SOME OF THE SO-CALLED BRIGHTEST MINDS OF OUR TIME.[2]

—RAVI ZACHARIAS

David Wells graphically compares our day to a mighty rolling tide that surges on unabated. And we are inescapably a part of it, tossed about like small corks on the ocean surface, driven by great swelling forces over which we appear to have no control.

This mighty surging flood, Wells claims, is bringing about fundamental changes throughout the world. Modern philosophies have stirred to a frenzy the relentless assault on all of the old certainties, both religious and moral.

Virtually all moral absolutes and most religious beliefs disappear in this raging flood. Cut loose from the old bonds, we spring forth as revolutionaries, prophets in a new millennium of unbelief, sages in a new world that has no horizons and recognizes only one god—possibility.[3]

The Western world, once the custodian of truth and a stable moral order, has become like a flock of swooping bats whose silent, unpredictable flight in the new civilization is an omen of "something gone dreadfully wrong."[4] What thinking person would disagree with Wells?

What drives this great moving tide? What is shaping this new civilization? It is not powerful truths or great ideas, or even a transcendent vision of reality. In the past ideas counted, but in our time they do not.

Human beings no longer view truth as a fixed reality, as unchanging absolutes. A single area of modern experience—specifically, science—drives this obsession with progress. Moderns hope for a world made over by technology. The prospects of conquering disease, discomfort, and distance loom large in the desire for limitless improvement. Such belief in progress gives us an aura of immortality.[5]

Without doubt, our fixation on progress has severed our ties to community, to church, to family, and to our own convictions. It has cut us loose from what held us in the past, making us vulnerable to all kinds of insidious and powerful forces.

THE CHURCH'S RESPONSE

What does the Christian church have to say about the world and even the church being reshaped into an uncertain future? Many denominations respond like the proverbial frog in the kettle. Because the water temperature rises slowly, the frog fails to sense the danger until it is too late.

However, that was not the case with the apostolic church. The first Christians knew their faith to be absolutely true. Consequently, they brooked no rivals and sought no compromises. In early church history their sure and certain conviction about truth powered the phenomenal growth described in the biblical book appropriately called the Acts of the Apostles.

Millions converted to Christianity by and because of "an unchanging gospel handed down by pen and mouth from age to age, generation to generation, mother to child, teacher to taught, pulpit to pew . . . that which had been believed in every place and every community by all Christian men and women."[6]

84

DEFINING TRUTH

The perils of the modern world challenge us to define and thus embrace the truth given to the Christian church and held so tenaciously through the ages. Without doubt, early Christian faith embraced the doctrinal truths found in Scripture. To be a believer in the New Testament meant accepting what the apostles taught. This led the Christian church to frame and preserve its beliefs in doctrinal terms. There can be no Christian faith in the absence of sound doctrine (1 Tim. 1:10; Titus 1:9). It is this doctrine—or more precisely, the truth it contains and expresses—that the apostles taught and delivered to the church. This message of truth is our only ground for hope (Titus 1:9) and salvation (1 Cor. 15:2; 1 Peter 1:23-25).

The Word of God—the Old Testament scriptures and the Word of God coming through the apostles—occupied central place in the life of the New Testament church. After all, Jesus' sole and final authority had been the Scriptures (Matt. 4:4). Paul admonished Timothy, and through him all other pastors, to preach nothing else but the truths revealed in Scripture (2 Tim. 4:1-4). The church is to be the pillar and ground of truth (1 Tim. 3:15). However, today the swelling tide of modern philosophies and ideas threatens the biblical foundations of truth. How are we to understand truth?

DIFFERING VIEWS OF TRUTH

A friend trying to move me from my biblical understanding of truth argued that "the teaching found in the Bible, rather than being the infallible Word of God, reflects the views held by the culture in which the writer lived." Consequently, he believed many of its teachings, especially Paul's, to be biased, bigoted, and unchristian. He further argued that the concept of a supernatural communication from God of the "right ideas" or of "fixed truth" with an absolute and eternal value is impossible.

My friend was actually reflecting Immanuel Kant's concept of epistemological doubt. Kant's argument caters to the colored glasses idea. According to Kant, the "colors" we see are not in the things seen, but are part of our own perception. What we claim to see in the Bible is not truth or reality, but simply *our* understanding of reality. This view holds that while absolute truth may exist, it can never be framed by human constructions or statements. Consequently, we are told, human beings can never know truth with any degree of certainty.

A second idea, driven by evolution, views truth not as a fixed idea or concept, but rather a dynamic, fluid conception always evolving to something new and different, thus invalidating the old. Those who hold this view define this "process" as the "truth." It applies an antitheistic scientific method of research, with naturalistic presuppositions, to the study of the Word of God. Today this method appears to be doing for religious studies what it has already done for scientific studies, namely, freeing them from any fixed understanding of truth.[7]

The third view claims that there is truth and that we can find it in natural law through unaided human logic and reason. This concept of truth results ultimately in relativism and a pluralistic understanding simply because we have no objective base to which we can appeal.

If we must establish truth by human logic and reason, then whose logic or reason is correct? And let's not be so naive as to think that the church (or for that matter, society) does not need some objective authority to which we can appeal. Because people cannot live in unity and harmony without authority, many place the church in the seat of authority. The Catholic Church is more realistic than some Protestants in admitting our need for objective authority.

The fourth concept holds that we can know truth because God supernaturally reveals it to the human race. Thus truth is fixed and infallible. While there will be enlargement and amplification, the new will not contradict the old. Let me be quick to state that the affirming of absolute truth must not negate the necessary role of logic and reason in its discovery and study. However, human reason must not become the final court of appeals.

Jesus belonged to this latter perspective. Most Christians have in the past subscribed to this concept of truth. Editor William Johnsson confirms this position when he writes: "While our understanding of truth is progressive, truth never contradicts itself. 'New light' cannot deny 'old light.' . . . New light amplifies and clarifies, never nullifies the old."[8]

JESUS' VIEW OF TRUTH

Jesus taught that we can know truth and know it well enough to even govern our lives by it. He said: "Man shall not live by bread alone, but by every word that proceedeth out of the mouth of God" (Matt. 4:4). How could we possibly believe or order our lives in harmony with a truth that we cannot understand?

What then is truth?

Jesus is the truth. He said: "I am the way, the truth, and the life." Jesus is a revelation of the true reality all are searching for. In Him we find hid "all the treasures of wisdom and knowledge" (Col. 2:3). His life and work demonstrated what God is like. As He told His disciple Philip: "He that hath seen me hath seen the Father" (John 14:9). So in Jesus Christ we can know the truth about God. We grasp the reality of God.

What Jesus taught constituted truth. He says, "Whoever hears these sayings of Mine, and does them, I will liken him to a wise man who built his house on the rock: and the rain descended, the floods came, and the winds blew and beat on that house; and it did not fall, for it was founded on the rock. Now everyone who hears these sayings of Mine, and does not do them, will be like a foolish man who built his house on the sand: and rain descended, the floods came, and the winds blew and beat on that house; and it fell. And great was its fall" (Matt. 7:24-27, NKJV).

What Jesus did is truth. His every work revealed the reality that God holds in store for each of us, what He will do for us if we only believe. The miracles that He performed were more than some psychological awakening by the person healed. They were supernatural restorations of bodies and minds. And they demonstrated the omnipotence of God's power and testified to the fact that Jesus was God in human flesh. Also, they pointed to the future reality that awaits all who will respond to God's compassionate and gracious love.

Finally, what Jesus believed is the truth. Jesus accepted the full inspiration of the Old Testament, including the worldview in Genesis, with its literal description of the Creation, Adam and Eve, the Garden of Eden, the temptation and Fall, and the Flood. I don't know of any significant scholar who denies this. And if we do not allow Jesus to define truth for us, then our claim to be Christians is not only nonsense but outright dishonesty.

A PROBLEM

But many sincere individuals find accepting these simple truths difficult. The Roman governor Pilate, during Christ's trial, struggled with a similar problem. However, Jesus said that if we are willing, we will know whether a doctrine is from God or whether it is a human creation (John 7:17). Anyone who is honest and sincere and comes to the Word of God in faith will pierce through the darkness, grasp the light of truth, and know that His Word is truth.

Of course, we will always struggle with questions. Apparent contradictions and difficult problems remain. However, they need not cause one person to lose faith in the Word of God.

A DANGER TO AVOID

Pursuing a purely intellectual objective in our study and research, even of the Bible, constitutes a stumbling block for many today who seek after knowledge. The student and scholar may not share a genuine longing to participate in the realities he or she discovers. Such individuals search for knowledge and data, but not for transformation. Acquiring knowledge has become an end in itself. Consequently, they are totally oblivious to the spiritual realities to which their new knowledge should lead. Lacking a genuine touch with reality, they persevere in asking why instead of how we should respond to this new truth. And they remain "eternal spectators,"[9] never experiencing the presence of God or the renewing power of His Spirit.

BENEFITS OF KNOWING THE TRUTH

Truth assures us of life's richest blessings by bringing us into contact with objective reality, with the way things actually are. Being spiritual creatures, human beings are able, through truth, to participate in the reality of the world around them, not merely in the sense of exerting an influence on that world, but in an intentional relationship through spiritual and intellectual apprehension of the truth about that world.

Truthful knowledge equips human beings to penetrate to the essence and quality of things. And more important, by acquiring a knowledge of things, they are able to possess them. Human beings have been given a unique consciousness of physical and spiritual realities above all the rest of creation, a sovereign status that reflects the image of the Creator-God in them.

This sure and certain knowledge supplies a base for our emotions, volitions, and conduct. Without an underlying knowledge of reality, we could not be affected and enriched by the values we find inherent in this reality.

The knowledge we find in Christ and the Scriptures enables us to know God—to form concepts of Him, His character, His love, and His work for us. Truthful knowledge enables us to grasp what God would have us be and what the future will be like in the life to come after our transformation.

Further, truthful knowledge brings us into a vital relationship with this God who reveals Himself in truth. In fact, the principal purpose of knowledge is to allow us to enter into relationship with the only true and living God, who is the truth. Then we participate with Him in His reality. We are able to contemplate Him "eye-to-eye,"[10] as it were—to adore Him, and to immerse ourselves in His love. Thus His streams of love flow into our own lives, wooing us further into that intimate relationship with God that only the Christian can know. This intimate union, the true wedlock of oneness with God, is the key to the greatest joy and fulfillment we can ever possibly know. It brings us a growing certainty of the reality of God, of His power, of His love for us, and of His watchcare over us. Truthful knowledge forms the indispensable foundation for union with God.

Such knowledge alone can bring us a true and lasting sense of meaning and purpose. We see our place and work in the context of the whole of things. Only the Christian can, in the fullest sense, have a true vision of reality, of God, and of the supernatural realm from which everything derives its ultimate meaning.

CONCLUSION

The steadfastness of our commitment to live in the light of the Christian revelation determines the degree of meaning and purpose that we will experience in life.

Coming to know the truth and entering into a dynamic relationship with the living God constitutes the essence of conversion. It is the process by which the Christian life awakens to an ever-increasing consciousness of eternal realities. Conversion itself allows us to understand everything in the context of our relationship to God and His truth.

In this relationship with God, the Christian finds an unshakable certainty about the issues of life. Even though we may feel like small corks bobbing on the ocean's surface, in danger of being swept away by the frightening world drama surging around us, nothing can move us! We find an anchor and rest in the shadow of a mighty, unmovable, eternal Rock.

---

[1] Dietrich von Hildebrand, *The New Tower of Babel,* p. 80.

[2] R. Zacharias, *Can Man Live Without God?* p. 122.

[3] D. Wells, *No Place for Truth,* p. 72.

[4] *Ibid.*

[5] *Ibid.,* p. 59.

[6] Owen Chadwick, *The Idea of Doctrinal Development* (New York: Cambridge University Press, 1957), p. 1.

[7] George M. Marsden, "God and Man at Yale," *First Things,* April 1994, p. 40.

[8] William Johnsson, "Present Truth," *Adventist Review,* Jan. 6, 1994, p. 9.

[9] Dietrich von Hildebrand, *Transformation in Christ* (Manchester, N.H.: Sophia Institute Press, 1948), p. 60.

[10] *Ibid.,* p. 59.

CHAPTER 9

THE ILLUSION OF PROGRESS

THE MOST ACCURATE CHART OF THE MEANING OF HISTORY IS A SET OF TRACKS MADE BY A DRUNKEN FLY, FEET WET WITH INK, STAGGERING ACROSS A PIECE OF WHITE PAPER, LEADING NOWHERE AND REFLECTING NO MEANING.
—AUTHOR UNKNOWN

TODAY WE CANNOT CLAIM TO KNOW THE END OF THE GOAL OF HISTORY; THERE-FORE, THE QUESTION OF MEANING IN HISTORY HAS BECOME MEANINGLESS.[1]
—RUDOLF BULTMANN

If the bloodletting in the twentieth century exemplifies all of history, then one would be inclined to agree with Hegel that history is nothing more than "a butcher's block."[2]

Few would deny that any meaning of history is hard to come by. The traditionalist finds significance only in the past and seeks to go back to what has been. The existentialist sees meaning only in the now and consequently lives for the present. The futurist or utopianist denies the significance of both the past and the present and looks only to the future for meaning, for the appearance of the new human beings who will bring universal peace.

However, without a proper framework in which to interpret history, we fail to make sense of all the flotsam and jetsam of personal and world events, happenings that engulf us all and often dictate the direction of our lives.

The framework within which we interpret what we read and observe we call a "belief system" or "worldview." Whether they realize it or not, everyone views the world and its happenings through some worldview that deeply influences their understanding of life and their response to events.

After I had presented a lecture on the biblical worldview, particularly the special Creation recorded in Genesis 1, a man from Nashville, Tennessee, confronted me with the argument that we don't have to interpret the days of the biblical Creation week as literal days. "That being the case," he said, "the concept of Creation in one literal week doesn't hold a drop of water."

"What makes you so sure that the days in Genesis are not literal 24-hour periods?" I responded.

"Science has proven that life developed over long periods of time. It couldn't have happened in one short week."

"Have you accepted an evolutionary worldview?" I queried.

"Absolutely not," came his quick response.

"Then what basis do you have for rejecting the biblical view of Creation?"

"Well," he said, "the days in Genesis represent long periods of time in which God, working through the laws of nature, created this planet and the diversity we find in it."

"Isn't that still evolution?" I persisted.

"No, if God did it, it's not evolution."

"I'm confused," I continued. "Do you mean God used evolution to create His universe?"

"Well," he hesitated, "it may be evolution; but it's not atheistic evolution." Without realizing it, this sincere man had exchanged his biblical worldview for a worldview interpreted by the theory of evolution. And it had radically altered his understanding of Christian truth.

Human beings use two basic worldviews, or belief systems, to interpret history.

THE SECULAR VIEW OF HISTORY

The first worldview, or belief system, we will briefly review sees Darwin's secular or atheistic evolution as the guiding principle and force driving history. This view leaves history, according to secular evolutionists, to the destiny of random chance and accidental development inherent in the evolutionary process itself. Faith in the laws and workings of nature provides the only explanation of life and the only hope for the future.

THE BIRTH OF THEISTIC EVOLUTION

Today the older secular winds that first drove the idea of evolutionary progress are gaining strength and mixing with the winds filling the sails of a surprising number of philosophical and theological ships. Thus a hybrid understanding of the evolutionary worldview has resulted.

Probably the most far-reaching consequence of the direction taken by these new theological ships is the replacement of both the atheistic evolutionary and biblical view of history with a theistic evolutionary perspective of the human race and its world. *Theos* is the Greek word for God. The expression "theistic evolution" then denotes a belief system that sees evolution as the means God uses to create all His works.

Much of Christianity has gradually bought into the theistic evolutionary worldview. Consequently, society has a strong belief in progress. This is the reason many regard the older Christian doctrines and practices as inferior or to be discarded. It leads to radical changes in every Christian doctrine, particularly the Christian view of history.

Pierre Teilhard de Chardin, a professing Christian theologian and the father of modern theistic evolution, pointed out that our worldview controls and changes our understanding not only of Christian teaching, but all of life. He writes: "Evolution is a light which illuminates all facts, a trajectory which all lines of thought must follow."[3]

Even evangelical theologians have widely accepted a theistic evolutionary view of our world. Zachery Hayes commented: "At the present time it would be true to say that some form of evolutionary theory is found to be acceptable to the mainstream of theologians and the major Christian traditions of the West."[4]

Brian Hebblethwaite, a representative contemporary theologian, supports this wide acceptance among evangelicals and argues that "the doctrines of Creation and providence can quite easily be reconciled with an evolutionary picture of the cosmos."[5] Anthony Campolo, a sociologist and popular evangelical speaker, is in the forefront of this new direction. He writes that through Jesus, God is "hominising not only man, but all of creation. Everything in heaven and earth is being gathered into the Christosphere. Salvation is the final result of cosmic evolution, which brings into being a new heaven and a new earth."[6] Campolo sees the future as an interdependent system of theology and evolution that makes "Christ integral to evolutionary development."[7]

Hebblethwaite reveals a dogged commitment of evangelicals to evolution when he writes that "whatever the problems with the theistic evolutionary view, we are not going to go back on the overall evolutionary picture or on the conception of man as emerging from very primitive conditions. . . . That Christian theology must now think in terms of a more or less gradual process from small beginnings right up to a perfected consummation in the future is beyond question of doubt."[8]

Such scholars claim that the biblical picture of the world after the Second Coming simply portrays the perfection of the earth during the final stage of evolution. It is difficult to accept such an evolutionary worldview without also embracing universalism. One author who openly espouses universalism says that "Christian faith and hope is the conviction that God's creation is moving toward an eternal consummation in which all men and all women from all ages will participate."[9] He argues that "the whole creative process must be thought of as being brought to a stage where there is no evil, deprivation, grief, or pain, and no falling away from perfection whatsoever."[10]

I asked one seminary professor who openly advocated evolution how he reconciled a doctrine of humanity created in the image of God with a theistic evolutionary worldview. "I haven't thought about it," he replied.

THE ILLUSION OF PROGRESS

What is the evidence, if any, that this utopian goal of evolution is being realized in history? Although many believe that they have been accumulating data that shows progress, we must ask ourselves if our world is really changing for the better. Are there real signs that we are moving toward utopia? Everything around us proves that just the opposite is true. We are skidding steadily toward the gutter, toward global chaos and destruction. What is happening all over the world graphically illustrates this reality. Current events in the developing countries certainly do.

My wife and I spent a few years as missionaries in central and west Africa. Rwanda was one of our favorite countries. There you find mountains, a pleasant climate, wild animal parks, and the famous silverback gorillas, which we had the opportunity to see.

When I was first introduced in Rwanda, my colleague Robert Peck, a local missionary who was more like the Hutus in stature, jokingly identified himself with the Hutu. Then because I am tall he laughingly introduced me as a Tutsi. The deadly silence that followed spoke volumes about the tensions that alienated the two tribes. It was then that I learned of the fierce hatred and longstanding warfare between them.

Soon after we left that beautiful country the tribal hatred broke out in the violent and murderous war of 1994. The African leader who translated for me, a Tutsi, along with his wife and four children, was chopped to death by the angry Hutus. Authoritative sources tell us that close to 1 million Rwandans perished in the violent conflict between the two warring tribes.

Chapters 1 and 2 of this book recorded the bleak picture of progress in the Western world. Mountains of evidence indite the whole concept of progress and corroborate the incontrovertible fact of decay in Eastern and Western Europe and on the American continent. Few if any would disagree that the twentieth century has been the bloodiest century in all of recorded history. While Christians do not deny that at times we may observe progress in history, few can maintain that humanity will attain its full destiny within secular history.

A CHRISTIAN OR BIBLICAL WORLDVIEW

The third worldview is that of Christianity, which teaches that the power and motivation for a meaningful and productive life are inextricably linked to faith in God as revealed in Jesus Christ. Further, the Christian religion rests upon a particular knowledge of God, a knowledge revealed in history and inseparable from historical knowledge.

In fact, the essential articles of the Christian faith, while revealed in Scripture, are validated in history. Christianity and Judaism are the only truly historical religions. Christianity, then, because of its further fulfillment and confirmation in history, justifiably lays claim to being the only true religion.

CHRISTIAN FAITH AND MEANING

While intelligently observing world events can give us some understanding of history, we can gain a full understanding best in the light of revelation. Faith in a loving Creator-God opens a perspective of history illuminated by God's wisdom and purposes and clearly validated by reliable scientific evidence.

Christian history has as its framework a chronological system, with divine-ordained events at definite points. Beginning with Creation, its central point is the incarnation, suffering, death, and resurrection of Christ at His first coming. Its primary future point is the second coming of Christ. The Bible writers validated this reality by their focus and dependence on prophecy.

Without a Christian worldview it may appear that the direction of history depends upon random chance or the caprice of human activity. However, "in the Word of God the curtain is drawn aside, and we behold, behind, above, and through all the play and counterplay of human interests and power and passions, the agencies of the all-merciful One, silently, patiently working out the counsels of His own will." [11]

At the time of the Creation God pronounced the earth, human beings, and all creation good and perfect. However, that quickly changed. The new creation took a wrong turn, shifting humanity onto a collision course with the terrible consequences erupting from its violation of God's moral laws. That crash shattered the Edenic perfection. Atrophy and degeneration of the spiritual, moral, and social life followed. Moral depravity, with its corollary of violence and death, soon wrecked the earth.

A prophecy found in Daniel 2 also affirms the downward degenerative direction of history, providing a stark contrast to the scientific worldview called evolution. The prophet Daniel predicts and describes this downward plight of humanity in his prophecy of the great image representing the four great world empires of history: Babylon, 605 to 538 B.C.; Persia, 508 to 331 B.C.; Greece, 331 to 168 B.C.; and Rome, 168 B.C. to A.D. 476. The prophecy concludes with the image's feet and toes of iron mixed with clay, representing the disunity and conflict from the fall of the Roman Empire to the end of history.

Finally a stone cut out without hands strikes the image in the feet, destroys it, and becomes a mountain that fills the whole earth. Jesus compared the end of the world to the events taking place at the time of the Flood and to the destruction of Sodom (Luke 17:26-29).

According to this prophecy, world conditions will continue to grow progressively worse until it comes to a crisis point in which God (the stone cut out without hands, representing the second coming of Christ) must intervene in order to save the world from total destruction. Ravi Zacharias is one of many contemporary Christian apologists who accept the validity of this prophecy, written 500 years before Christ. He identifies the third kingdom in the prophecy as the Greece of Alexander the Great and the fourth as the empire of pagan Rome.[12] He also uses Jesus' prophecies in Matthew 24 to describe the future as a time of great trouble moving toward the "latter days."[13]

Obviously Jesus Himself affirms this downward spiral of human history. When asked about the time of the end, He assured His disciples that just as signs tell when spring is near, so there will be indications when God will again break into human history (Matt. 24). His description of those signs reads like the daily newspaper—earthquakes, famines, war, and strife.

WHAT THEN OF THE FUTURE?

World conditions will grow continually worse. Even though we work for a better and more secure future, we will not realize our dreams before Christ returns. Natural and human-made disasters, poverty, hunger, disease, racial strife, national conflicts, and war will increasingly plague the world. Jesus predicted more moral and social problems, such as the deterioration of the family, strained relations between children and parents, and more violence and crime. We can expect great economic difficulties, prejudice, hostility, and persecution around the world, particularly in the area of religion.

World leaders have already begun to turn to the churches for help in resolving the world's problems. This will result in a religiopolitical system of government. World conditions, however, will still continue to deteriorate to the point of self-destruction.

But history does not end in a nuclear conflagration resulting in a global meltdown. Instead, the return of Christ will begin a new history with a bright future. Some interpretations of history seem to expect perfection within history. That was the message of Communism. However, Jesus said, "I make all things new" (Rev. 21:5).

John the revelator saw our world replaced by a new one (verses 1-3). No hellish wars between Serbs and Croatians, Hutus and Tutsis, Arabs and Jews, East and West. No weapons of war will spill the blood of the citizens of this new society. No AIDS virus, no hunger, no broken families, no child abuse, no senseless suicide, no murder of unborn babies, will ever be recorded in the history books of God's new world.

CONCLUSION

History then is pregnant with meaning and purpose. It is much more than Shakespeare's "tale told by an idiot, full of sound and fury, signifying nothing." What then is history's meaning? It is both the unfolding of a great conflict between good and evil and the outworking of a loving God to win back a world under the control of a fallen angel called Lucifer.

The Christian view of history clearly reveals the work of a loving and redemptive Creator God. The evil we find in history, described by Hegel as a "butcher's block," points to Satan, the fallen Lucifer. All of history demonstrates both the nature of evil and the justice and benevolence of God in all His dealings with humanity. In addition, it shows the lofty and unchanging nature of God's government, His moral laws, and the results of violating those eternal principles.

The Christian sees secular history as really salvation history. It is the tale of human rebellion and God's redemptive love in sending His own Son to pay the debt humanity owed and bring us back home. Christians experience meaning in history because they know that all of history, including their lives, is under the control of the God who is silently and patiently working out His own will.

Is history like the tracks of a drunken fly stumbling across a sheet of white paper, leading nowhere and meaning nothing? No. It is an arrow shot from a powerful bow by an expert archer, speeding inexorable toward its God-ordained destination, where God's will at last fully achieves His purposes in creating humanity and its world.

---

[1] Rudolf Bultmann, *The Presence of Eternity: History and Eschatology* (New York: Harper and Row, 1957), pp. 97-111.

[2] Quoted in *First Things*, August/September 1994, p. 18.

[3] Quoted in Ken Ham, *The Lie* (El Cajon, Calif.: Creation-Life Publishers, 1973), p. 16.

[4] Z. Hayes, *What Are They Saying About Creation?* p. 53.

[5] Brian Hebblethwaite, *The Christian Hope* (Grand Rapids: William B. Eerdmans Pub. Co., 1984), p. 123.

[6] Anthony Campolo, *A Reasonable Faith* (Waco, Tex.: Word, 1983), p. 65.

[7] *Ibid.*

[8] *Ibid.*

[9] Hebblethwaite, p. 199.

[10] *Ibid.*, p. 224.

[11] E. G. White, *Education*, p. 173.

[12] Zacharias, *Can Man Live Without God?* p. 156.

[13] *Ibid.*, p. 176.

WHAT DIFFERENCE DOES IT MAKE?

A MAGNIFICENT OBSESSION

WHENEVER SOME HIGH GOOD IN OUR LIFE APPEARS THREATENED—A BELOVED PERSON, FOR INSTANCE, HAS FALLEN GRAVELY ILL OR OUR OWN LIFE IS IN DANGER—WE AT ONCE BECOME AWARE OF THE PETTINESS AND FUTILITY OF ALL THOSE PALTRY THINGS TO WHICH WE HAVE FORMERLY ATTACHED SO GREAT IMPORTANCE. HOW WILLINGLY WOULD WE RENOUNCE ALL OF THEM, IF ONLY WE COULD THEREBY SAVE THAT ONE PRECIOUS GOOD. . . . THIS LIBERATING POWER OF A HIGH VALUE OR A DEEP EXPERIENCE IS MOST STRIKINGLY MANIFESTED WHENEVER A PERSON'S HEART IS INFLAMED WITH A NOBLE PASSION OF LOVE.[1]

—DIETRICH VON HILDEBRAND

I CHALLENGE A NEW GENERATION OF YOUNG AMERICANS TO A SEASON OF SERVICE—TO ACT ON YOUR IDEALISM BY HELPING TROUBLED CHILDREN, KEEPING COMPANY WITH THOSE IN NEED, RECONNECTING OUR TORN COMMUNITIES. THERE IS SO MUCH TO BE DONE—ENOUGH INDEED FOR MILLIONS OF OTHERS WHO ARE STILL YOUNG IN SPIRIT TO GIVE THEMSELVES IN SERVICE TOO.[2]

—BILL CLINTON

EVERY SINGLE ANCIENT WISDOM AND RELIGION WILL TELL YOU THE SAME THING: DON'T LIVE ENTIRELY FOR YOURSELF; LIVE FOR OTHER PEOPLE. DON'T GET STUCK INSIDE YOUR OWN EGO, BECAUSE IT WILL BECOME A PRISON IN NO TIME FLAT.[3]

—BARBARA WARD

Jack Lynch came to his calling in a strange way. Originally from Illinois, he had served in World War II and was a bush pilot, a demolitionist, a prospector in Mexico, and finally, a construction worker in Milwaukee. However, he was always restless and uneasy. Life held little meaning. In 1960 he read a magazine article about a Dr. E. H. McCleary, who lived in Pennsylvania and raised lobo wolves—the true American wolf.

In 1920 Dr. McCleary had become concerned that the wolves would be totally exterminated and the species lost forever. He purchased 25 live-trapped lobos and kept them on a farm outside Kane, Pennsylvania.

"I can't explain it," Lynch said, "but I felt this was something I had to know about. I took off work and drove straight to Kane." McCleary was 93 when Lynch met him. He found McCleary impoverished, ill, feeble, and gnawed by worry about what would become of the lobos when he was gone.

"Within minutes," Lynch said, "I was absolutely sure that taking care of the wolves would give my life some meaning. I had never seen anything, no other animal or human, that moved me as much as they."

He returned to Milwaukee, sold the property he owned there, quit his job, and in 1961 returned to Pennsylvania, where he purchased some of McCleary's farmland and all 32 of his wolves for $1,000 each. Lynch spent more than 25 years living with, caring for, and guarding these magnificent animals.

Throughout his life he religiously concerned himself with the fate of these most renowned of all North American wolves, the great lobo, or buffalo wolf. "Before I came to the wolves, I was like a lot of people. I couldn't name one thing I had done that was worth anything to anybody but myself, that would have any meaning after I was gone. Now I have saved the genes of the buffalo wolves. I am part of the future whether anybody remembers my name or not. I believe that my life has been worth living. I don't envy any man."[4]

Some of the great people of the past have been men and women who have discovered the joy of giving: David Livingstone, beloved missionary to Africa; William Booth, founder of the Salvation Army; Florence Nightingale, pioneer in nursing the mentally ill; and Mother Teresa, who has spent her life caring for the rejected orphans of India.

This principle of giving finds its motive and power in the life and teaching of Jesus. "Give," Jesus said, "and it shall be given unto you; good measure, pressed down, and shaken together, and running over" (Luke 6:38).

FREEING AND AWAKENING THE SOUL

If we refuse to give, we shut up and close the door to every blessing available to humanity. It stops up the wells of fulfillment and satisfaction, bringing in its wake confusion, dissatisfaction, disease, and death. William Menninger, respected psychologist and one of the founders of the famed Menninger Clinic in Topeka, Kansas, recognized the evil result of putting self first. Menninger acknowledged that hatred, the spoiled fruit of selfishness, is "the root of all mental illness."[5]

However, when people break free from the destructive power of selfishness and begin to express a real concern for others by giving of themselves, their time, and their resources, then that act of giving looses and frees the soul. It touches and awakens the godlikeness in human beings and releases all the latent powers the Creator gave to the human race at Creation. To give is to become conscious of life and awakens a new awareness of one's high destiny.

Most of the world has forgotten that giving brings happiness, joy, longevity, and health. Once it is rediscovered, it will bring renewal to the individual and to the church. The more a person gives, the more he or she wants to give.

One of the great religious writers of history writes of this reality: "The law of love calls for the devotion of body, mind, and soul to the service of God and our fellowman. And this service, while making us a blessing to others, brings the greatest blessing to ourselves."[6]

Unselfishness underlies all true development. Through unselfish service we develop every faculty to its highest. More and more fully we become partakers of the divine nature. Unselfishness fits us for heaven, for we receive heaven into our hearts.

Stanley Kresge speaks of this concept when he acknowledges that money is important, but not the most important thing. "Have no illusions about the power of money. But it is silly to dismiss it as worthless. It means many good things. It represents dormitories, classrooms, hospitals. It represents research facilities and the priceless efforts of men and women of creative skills and genius. But money alone cannot build character or transform evil into good. It cries for full partnership with leaders of character and good will, who value good tools and the creation and enlargement of life for man, who was created in the image of God."[7]

I believe this is what it means to be born again or re-created in the image of God.

Woodrow Wilson, when president of Princeton, said of the principle of self-forgetting service: "Nothing but what you volunteer has the essence of life, the springs of pleasure in it. These are the things you do because you want to do them, the things that your spirit has chosen for its satisfaction. The more you are stimulated to such action, the more clearly does it appear to you that you are a sovereign spirit put into the world, not to wear harness but to work eagerly without it."[8]

The law of giving is as well a sound principle of psychology. William Menninger underscores this principle: "For maturity everyone has to have a cause, a mission, an aim in life, that is constructive and so big that they keep working at it. It is a mental health practice to find a mission that is so much bigger than you are that you can never accomplish it alone—a mission for the common good, a mission that takes thought and energy. . . . This is part of emotional maturity and I would strongly urge that if you have no mission you find one."[9]

Here we have the central truth of biblical religion. In the beginning all God's creation existed to give. Nothing lived to itself. Human beings and animals lived to minister to some other life. Even today the trees, shrubs, and flowers breathe out life-giving oxygen and delightful fragrances, and unfold their beauty in blessing to the world. The sun sheds its light to gladden our world. The ocean itself is the source of all our springs and rivers. Even the angels find their joy in giving. Giving, then, is the great spiritual principle of life. If practiced, life results—but if ignored, death follows quickly.

It was Lucifer, an angel whose name means light bearer, who first introduced the law of selfishness or self-exaltation into the universe. Rather than living to serve others, he chose to exalt himself. We see his self-centeredness in his goals: "I will ascend into heaven, I will exalt my throne above the stars of God: I will sit also upon the mount of the congregation, in the sides of the north: I will ascend above the heights of the clouds; I will be like the most High" (Isa. 14:13, 14).

Today we know too well the results of selfishness: unhappiness, misery, strife, war, and death. And yet the world generally accepts this law and practices it. This is why Jesus came to reveal that it is the glory of God to give. Jesus, by coming to earth, showed us a better way: the way of self-forgetting service that leads to all the blessings promised to humanity. Notice again Jesus' words: "Give, and it shall be given unto you; good measure, pressed down, and shaken together." Giving, then, is the law of life. In fact, giving is the primary focus of the Ten Commandments. Jesus summed them up in two simple but profound concepts: loving service to God and loving service to humanity (see Matt. 22:37-40).

The McKees of McKee Foods, headquartered at Collegedale, Tennessee, have from the beginning of their business life practiced these two laws. Going the second mile, they added a practice expressed by John Wesley: "Make all the money you can and then give away as much as you can." [10]

We find our joy in loving service to God and to humanity. True religion is, as John Wesley said, " faith working by love." The following quote reveals Wesley's service-oriented understanding of Christianity: "Repentance is the porch of religion, faith is the door, and loving service is religion itself." Elsewhere he said that "the gospel of Christ knows no religion but social, no holiness but social holiness. Faith working by love is the length and breadth, the depth and height of Christian perfection." [11]

Dan and Kathy Blackburn, natives of rural Indiana, understood this principle of Christianity when in 1977 they opened a Christian missionary school for children in the remote Haitian village of Maissade. It was their dream that through education they could break the cycle of violence, poverty, and despair that trapped the children of Haiti almost from the day they were born.

Initially the Blackburns concentrated on the school and on reaching out to people. However, one evening an old woman, with the dust of Haiti's mountain paths clinging in stark whiteness to her deep black skin, came to the back door of their house. She clutched to her thin chest a bundle of dirty rags. Dan turned and said to Chuck, his 11-year-old son, who was with him at the back of the house, "I think she has a sick baby." [12]

They quickly saw that the child was near death. When they told the old woman there was nothing they could do, she became frantic. Her voice beseeching, she thrust the dirty bundle into Chuck's arms. "Please, please take the baby," she cried. She told them the mother had died immediately after giving birth. The grandmother had no place to take the baby but to the Blackburns. The woman explained to Kathy

Blackburn that she was the only person on earth who cared about this baby, and that she herself was sick and dying. Unable to resist, Kathy took the baby, a boy, and they named him Toma.[13]

Less than one month after the family began caring for Toma, a blue-suited Tonton Macoute, a member of a murderous group of thugs, appeared at their gate. As Kathy came to the door, the man thrust a bundle toward her. "You take babies here?" he asked in Creole. He said he was the father and that the mother had died in birth.

Kathy told her husband, "I don't know how we can take care of another child." But even as she said it, she reached for the baby. They named him Sam and put him in a makeshift bed alongside Toma.

Soon word got around in the village and surrounding area. Not long afterward 6-month-old Jim Bob, whose body was terribly swollen because of inadequate protein, joined the first two infants. The child was simply starving to death.

A special bonding began taking place between the Blackburns and the babies. Next someone brought a little girl. They named her Cheryl. Others came, and soon they had nine children.

Every passing year they received other children, whom they named Robert, Yvonne, Rebeka, Rosie, Mary, Stephen, Marva, Jeremiah, Noah, Aaron, Gideon, Elizabeth, Benjamin, JoAnna, Abigail, Jacob, Jemima, Rachel, Thaddeus, Caleb, Matthew, Michael, Mark, and Andy. Eventually 28 children packed every nook and corner of the small Blackburn residence.

Raising 28 children put tremendous pressure and stress on the Blackburn family. However, when a crisis came, they always turned to God. Every time He gave them wisdom and new strength.

In 1986 a violent anti-American spirit erupted in Haiti, threatening not only the work of the Blackburn family but also their lives. The authorities told them that unless they left they would all be killed. Their only hope was to flee immediately to the neighboring Dominican Republic. Using a borrowed vehicle, they packed the 28 Haitian children, 17 boys and 11 girls, in the back of the truck. The Blackburn family squeezed themselves in the front. Miraculously they managed to get through all the checkpoints and finally arrived safely in the Dominican Republic, where they remained under asylum for 20 months.

Finally a friend contacted American Airlines, which agreed to fly them out of the country. On December 18, 1989, the Blackburn family, with all 28 of the Haitian children, arrived at Miami airport. In America they settled down in Elizabethtown, Indiana, to raise the 28 newly adopted children.

Despite the bedlam created by 20 teenagers, the Blackburns continue to find fulfillment in rearing their large family. Not only did Dan and Kathy Blackburn discover the greatest sense of meaning and purpose in their special ministry; the children also have experienced similar joy and happiness. Toma, the first of the children taken in, has grown tall and is powerfully built. When asked what it has been like growing up as one of 28 children, Toma squeezes his mother's arm and says, "All I know is that there has never been a day in my life that I have been unloved, not a day." [14]

If you want to live, you too must give. Give of yourself, your time, your energies, and your financial resources. Saving lobo wolves may not be your cup of tea, but how about your family, your country, your church, or possibly the destitute family down the street? For Mother Teresa it was the poor children of India, for Abraham Lincoln it was his country. The education of her children provided the purpose that challenged Susanna Wesley. The Blackburns found their mission in saving the infants of Haiti. For the apostle Paul it was his church. What magnificent obsession will make your life worth living?

---

[1] D. von Hildebrand, *Transformation in Christ,* p. 102.

[2] Quoted in *Words of Wisdom* (Silver Spring, Md.: Philanthropic Service for Institutions, 1993), p. 129.

[3] *Ibid.,* p. 128.

[4] Bill Gilbert, "The Wolf Man of Discovery Bay," *Sports Illustrated,* Nov. 5, 1979.

[5] William C. Menninger, *Living in a Troubled World* (Kansas City, Mo.: Hallmark Editions, 1967), p. 56.

[6] E. G. White, *Education,* p. 16.

[7] *Words of Wisdom,* p. 194.

[8] *Ibid.,* p. 181.

[9] Menninger, p. 53.

[10] Leon O. Hynson, *To Reform a Nation* (Grand Rapids: Francis Asbury Press, 1984), p. 48.

[11] *Ibid.,* p. 56.

[12] *Reader's Digest,* July 1995, p. 173.

[13] *Ibid.,* pp. 173, 174.

[14] *Ibid.,* pp. 174-199.

RAGS AND TATTERS

THE ANCHORAGE THAT THE INTERNAL WORLD OF THE SPIRIT HAD FOUND IN THE
SUPERNATURAL ORDER DISAPPEARED IN THE BLAZE OF ENLIGHTENMENT ATTITUDES,
AND THE SELF, NOW LEFT COMPLETELY TO ITSELF, CUT OFF FROM GOD AND FROM THE
OUTSIDE WORLD, BEGAN TO DISAPPEAR. ONCE SEVERED FROM THE LARGER FRAME-
WORKS OF MEANING, PEOPLE BECAME INCREASINGLY INTROSPECTIVE AND WHAT THEY
GAZED UPON LOOKED INCREASINGLY WEIGHTLESS.[1]
—DAVID B. WELLS

Bryan Wilson claims that Western civilization has abandoned the moral values that used to hold people together in a secure and meaningful society. Consequently, a cold winter chill has fallen over Western civilization, and all we have to cover ourselves with is a few "rags and tatters."[2]

He is not alone in his analysis. Solzhenitsyn described the moral condition of Western civilization as "a world split apart" that may not survive. Carl F. Henry writes of the "twilight of a great civilization" resulting from a rejection of the teaching of Christianity, which once provided the moral foundation for Western culture.[3]

The fraying of America's moral fabric—once considered the crotchety preoccupation of the fundamentalists—has become a national (even liberal) obsession. From the East Side of Manhattan to West Los Angeles, many Americans agree that there are universally accepted principles of good character and that society is failing to teach them anymore. In a 1994 *Newsweek* poll 76 percent of adults agreed that the United States is in moral and spiritual decline.[4] "No one today lives by the rules we were raised on," said one suburban mother. What happened to decency and respect?

However, the breakdown of the family, the school, and the government is stirring up new winds that many believe will turn the tide of evil and reestablish an old morality. The craving for virtue goes beyond the debate over whose values are best—traditional families or single parents, gays or straights, Jews or Christians, Black or White. Our growing awareness of the importance of morals has uncovered the painful fact that none of the traditional institutions are effectively teaching morals or positively affecting the moral behavior of our youth.

Parents are absent or busy. Neighbors no longer know each other. Mother is long gone from the home, replaced by Madonna music videos. Even religious institutions often seem more concerned with group grievances than individual behavior. Baby boomers, facing mortality and the even more frightening prospect of teenage kids, are waking up to the fact that there is at least one absolute after all: good character.

According to *Newsweek* magazine, all of the core institutions that once transmitted oral education are in disrepair. The family has fractured, neighborhoods have disappeared or turned surly, many schools can barely educate, and even many churches wonder what to teach. "You can't have strong virtues without strong institutions," says Jean Bethke Elshtain, professor of political science at Vanderbilt University.[5]

And key to this issue is the fact that you can't have strong institutions without an authoritative source that defines morality and its behavior.

TAKING A STAND

In 1992 a group of educators and philosophers met in the mountains of Colorado and produced something they called the Aspen Declaration. It listed six core elements of character that all youth-influencing institutions should stress: trustworthiness (including honesty and loyalty), respect, responsibility (including self-discipline and hard work), fairness, caring (compassion), and citizenship (including obeying laws, staying informed, and voting). Some believe, though, that you can be a virtuous person without faith in God.[6] (We will examine this idea later.)

William McGuffey, like other civic crusaders of his era, believed that government had to be actively involved in teaching goodness. Prominent educators and government leaders belong to this group.

They are all for character education in public schools—a trend already exploding across the country.[7]

However, despite the widespread call for virtue, we live in an age of moral relativism. According to the dominant school of moral philosophy, the skepticism engendered by an abuse of the Enlightenment and made acceptable by modern trends has reduced all ideas of right and wrong to matters of personal taste, emotional preference, or cultural choice. Since we cannot know ultimate truth, neither can we know what is truly good. Without agreed-upon social limits, people are free to make what they will of their private lives. And without a virtuous society, individuals cannot realize either their own or the common good. How do we fix the problem?

When young Abe Lincoln sought to educate himself, the immediately available and most obvious things to learn were the Bible, Shakespeare, and Euclid. In Lincoln's day the Bible functioned as a powerful educational tool. The religious culture of the nineteenth century grew out of a study of the Bible and provided the moral fabric of society. Moral teachings were religious ones.

Religious values were not something apart from the moral fabric that made up life itself. The meaning of life and the way one should live was incarnated in the biblical stories themselves. Growing out of this religious culture was a moral authority that guided both the individual and society itself.

However, today, with the acceptance of the so-called scientific or evolutionary worldview and the subsequent loss of faith in the biblical view of humanity, moral absolutes are no longer an integral part of our society. Today there is "a more or less open belief in progress, which means the past appears poor and contemptible. The future, which is open-ended, cannot be prescribed to by parents, and it eclipses the past, which they know to be inferior."[8] Moral truth has become an oxymoron.

Yet even nature itself teaches us that there is right and there is wrong. There is that which builds up and that which tears down. Ample evidence indicates that our rejection of the moral truths found in the Bible is the primary reason for modern society's moral confusion and its addiction to destructive behavior.

TRUTH AND FREEDOM

In the past we believed that freedom and truth were intricately interrelated. Today many have come to believe that freedom can get along without truth. However, that proposition is intellectually unconvincing, spiritually incoherent, and morally disastrous. When so-called truth becomes no more than the will of each individual, or even a majority of individuals, then society, the church, and the individual lose their moral compass.

When I commented about this fact to a friend whose destructive habits and immoral behavior were rapidly disintegrating his family, his career, and his health, he responded, "What difference does it make?"

Liberal views of truth have altered the very soil that nourishes the roots of Christian truth. While conservativism at times freezes truth, it at least effectively preserves the soil in which Christian faith and morality can, with clarification, grow to maturity.

The problem is that we each want to create our own truth. We want to decide for ourselves what is right and what is wrong, what is good and what is bad.

Today millions talk glibly about freedom. Freedom to explore, to discover what is right for them. And sexuality is usually at the center of the search. In most cases that quest ends in slavery rather than freedom, misery rather than happiness. As Allan Bloom says, freedom must always be tethered to truth. It cannot stand alone. If it does, it will degenerate into license.[9] If freedom is to be secured, it must always be accountable to truth. And only in Jesus can we know truth.

Jesus said that if we wish to enter into life, we should keep the commandments (Matt. 19:17). To find meaning and purpose in our lives requires a knowledge of truth. More than that, we must "do" truth. Life is ultimately fulfilled in following the One who said, "I am the way, the truth, and the life" (John 14:6).

Have you ever wondered why God framed His moral law of God in the negative? Could God have put it that way because we cannot always do the good we would? However, we can always refuse to do evil.[10]

When we break God's moral absolutes, evil results and pain and suffering follow. Since God is a moral God, He cannot ignore anything that hurts His creation. His government, then, must involve law, judgment, and justice.

WHY ACCEPT SOMEONE ELSE'S WORD?

The basis of our acceptance of moral absolutes is found in the truth that God is the Creator of all things. We human beings can discover security only as we recognize our dependence on God and on His wisdom and power. The covenant in the Garden of Eden of obey and live, disobey and die, was a valid one. As V. Norskov Olsen, university president, administrator, scholar, and theologian, says, "The covenant of life, more than a mere mandate or order, was a statement regarding the facts of the law-governed universe, a covenant that grew out of love, the very essence of God." [11]

Millions today are still learning that to obey is to live, while to disobey is to die. To interpret that statement only in the sense that God will punish us if we do not obey is to miss the point. God's laws all have a purpose. That purpose is to give life, to guarantee happiness, and to provide security. Meaning and purpose can be ours only as we recognize divine law. Our failure to conform to His moral principles will always result in alienation, pain, suffering, and death. God's judgments are not capricious. They are the natural consequences of violating the moral absolutes of divine law—of ultimate reality.

These moral laws regulate a moral universe just as physical laws guide the physical universe because God, a personal being and a moral lawgiver and ruler, made human beings in His own image. Humans are like God. They are moral beings because God is a moral God. Consequently, their inner convictions, their logic, and their reason testify to moral realities. When we evade and resist the voice of conscience, trouble, as a natural consequence, soon follows. Paul makes this point graphically when he expresses God's moral indignation toward sin rather than the sinner:

"For the wrath of God is revealed from heaven against all ungodliness and wickedness of men who by their wickedness suppress the truth. For what can be known about God is plain to them, because God has shown it to them. Ever since the creation of the world his invisible nature, namely, his eternal power and deity, has been clearly perceived in the things that have been made. So they are without excuse" (Rom. 1:18-20, RSV).

Not only do we observe the results of violating God's moral absolutes throughout human history; we also see them explicitly fulfilled in the life of Christ. Where we failed, He succeeded. He came not to do His own will, but the will of His heavenly Father. Christ becomes an example to us, showing us the way to life. This leads us to the fact that our relationship with God can be intimate and meaningful only as we recognize God's moral realities and endeavor, by the grace of God, to apply them to our lives.

If the law of God is a transcript of God's character, to go in a different direction will hinder and ultimately destroy our relationship with Him. Two people can walk together only as they agree. Keeping God's commandments is simply agreeing with Him. Herein lies the basis of all genuine fellowship with the moral God we see demonstrated in Jesus Christ.

The testimony of those who accept Christ as their personal Saviour validates this truth. "For the first time in my life," many exclaim, "I feel at peace with myself and with God."

Rejecting God's moral mandates will destroy not only ourselves, but society itself.

Recently the *Wall Street Journal*, referring to the collapse of moral values in our society, posited the idea that the biblical concept of sin is still valid and particularly true, it felt, in light of the explosion of sexually transmitted diseases following in the wake of the sexual revolution.

According to the *Journal*, "sin isn't something many people spent much time worrying about in the past 25 years. But we will say this for sin: it at least offered a frame of reference for behavior. . . . It now appears that many people could have used a road map." Referring to the problems of drugs, high school sex, AIDS, and rape, the editors stated unequivocally that "none of these will go away until people in positions of responsibility come forward and explain, in frankly moral terms, that some of the things people do nowadays are wrong."[12]

However, few in our morally unrestrained culture have seen the value of the prohibitions found in the Ten Commandments. How strange that a generation quick to grasp even the most questionable promises of modern technology, science, and medicine in the pursuit of a better life fails to see that God's law serves the same purpose. In face of the most convincing evidence—debilitating disease and the most dreadful forms of death—millions still fail to recognize the validity of the moral realities revealed in Jesus Christ.

Allan Bloom agrees and argues that a "life based on the Book [the Bible] is closer to the truth, that it provides the material for deeper research in and access to the real nature of things."[13] Particularly is this true when it comes to morality.

AN ALTERNATIVE?

The problem, obscured by a humanistic worldview, is that of the spiritual blindness of the human heart. Consequently, many moderns have difficulty seeing the practical and helpful wisdom contained in Christ's moral teachings.

Ted Turner's 10 "initiatives," which he set forth as more up-to-date and realistic directives for today's complicated world than the Ten Commandments, appear to underscore this fact. However, proclaiming the moral prohibitions of Scripture to the spiritually blind accomplishes about as much as cursing the darkness. Only as this blindness is removed can we see that the moral law is a hedge of love about us to protect us from harm. Only in the power of Christ can we overcome this blindness.

In teaching morality, the religious leadership of Christ's day focused on the externals of the law, thus failing to recognize the inherent motive of love. Consequently, when speaking of the law, Jesus had to describe it as a new commandment. His words in John 13:34 make it difficult to escape His emphasis: "A new commandment I give you: Love one another. As I have loved you, so you must love one another" (NIV). In Matthew 22:37-40 Jesus clearly interpreted the Ten Commandments in the context of love to God and love for others. Jesus set the law, not in the framework of strict and arbitrary demands, but in the warm atmosphere of loving, redemptive relationships. The strength of that love will more than fulfill the demands of the law.

It is sometimes difficult for us to understand why God gave the law at Sinai in such negative terms. However, when Christ came and spoke from another mountain, He turned two powerful spotlights on the law that illuminate it forever. Christ went far beyond the "don'ts" of the commandments. While He validated the moral prohibitions of the law, He further presented the commandments of God as beatitudes, blessings. When questioned as to the greatest commandment, He said, "Thou shalt love the Lord thy God with all thy heart. . . . Thou shalt love thy neighbour as thyself" (Mark 12:30). "There is none other commandment greater than these," He affirmed (verse 31).

It is in this context that the moral absolutes of God's Word provide the road map that could have protected this generation from the death and destruction following in the wake of the moral and sexual revolution.

God reminds us that our security and happiness grow out of obedience to the law. "If only you had paid attention to my commands, your peace would have been like a river, your righteousness like the waves of the sea" (Isa. 48:18). What then in His infinite wisdom does God require of us? "To do justly, and to love mercy, and to walk humbly with thy God" (Micah 6:8).

---

[1] D. B. Wells, *No Place for Truth,* p. 62.
[2] Quoted in Wells, p. 56.
[3] Carl F. Henry, *The Twilight of a Great Civilization* (Westchester, Ill.: Crossway Books, 1988), p. ix.
[4] *Newsweek,* June 13, 1994, p. 31.
[5] *Ibid.,* p. 39.
[6] *Ibid.*
[7] *Ibid.,* pp. 33, 36.
[8] Allan Bloom, *The Closing of the American Mind* (New York: Simon and Schuster, 1987), p. 58.
[9] *Ibid.*
[10] Richard John Newhouse, "The Splendor of Truth," *First Things,* January 1994, p. 15.
[11] V. N. Olsen, *Man, the Image of God,* p. 68.
[12] Daniel Henninger, "The Joy of What?" *Wall Street Journal,* Jan. 8, 1992.
[13] Bloom, p. 60.

CHAPTER 12

WHEN THE HAMMER FALLS

BELIEF IN A WORLD TO COME WHERE THE INNOCENT ARE COMPENSATED FOR THEIR SUFFERING CAN HELP PEOPLE ENDURE THE UNFAIRNESS OF LIFE IN THIS WORLD WITHOUT LOSING FAITH. BUT IT CAN ALSO BE AN EXCUSE FOR NOT BEING TROUBLED OR OUTRAGED BY INJUSTICE AROUND US, AND NOT USING OUR GOD-GIVEN INTELLIGENCE TO TRY TO DO SOMETHING ABOUT IT.[1]
—HAROLD S. KUSHNER

THAT WHICH DOES NOT KILL ME MAKES ME STRONGER.
—FRIEDRICH NIETZSCHE

A sense of foreboding shadowed my steps as I approached the nursing home where my mother resided while I was doing mission service in Africa. Entering the building, I could not find Mother. Her room was empty; nor did I locate her in the visiting area. The nurses' station assured me that Mother was in the visiting area.

Again I looked but could not find her. Back to the nurses' station. This time the nurse accompanied me briskly to the visiting area and pointed me toward a pathetic figure with long tangled hair hanging down over her face, neck, and shoulders. Her scanty clothing revealed a sheet rope strapping her in the chair.

Her upper torso appeared hinged at the waist as her head and shoulders swung down to the floor and then back up again into the chair. Up and down she moved, a distant and frightened look filling her eyes. Her mournful voice filled the room: "Mama, Mama, Mama."

This my mother? No, it could not be! Two years earlier she had been a charming and sensitive person.

Pulling a chair close to her side, I enclosed her hand in mine and began talking softly to her, hoping she would stop the swinging movement and plaintive crying. After about 20 minutes her movements slowed and then abruptly stopped. Almost as though nothing at all was wrong, she looked at me and said, "Why, John, is that you?" For a few brief moments we talked about family and friends. Then just as suddenly as Mother had broken out of the strange world that held her captive, the distant expression appeared once more, and she slipped into her strange, sad world. Her body resumed the same motions, and the plaintive cry again escaped her lips. Though desperately trying, I could not pierce the darkness and pain that imprisoned her.

Leaving the nursing home confused and angry, I questioned, Why should my mother, who had sacrificed everything to provide a Christian education for her five children, be allowed to suffer in this unthinkable way? She was the most faithful Christian I had ever known. Why should she have to endure such insult and pain? What of the promises that God would watch over His children and that no evil would befall them? A deep, aching sense of unfairness disturbed my mind and destroyed my peace. It just didn't make sense!

How could I square this with the promises of God?

Like many people, I was raised to believe that God was an all-wise, omnipotent heavenly Father who would treat us as our earthly parents did, or even better. He would reward us if we were good. If bad, He would discipline or punish us. Protecting us from being hurt or from hurting ourselves, He would see to it that we got what we deserved in life.

Throughout life I had been exposed to the human tragedies that shadow the landscape: close friends dying in tragic auto accidents, moral and upright people wasted by crippling diseases, innocent lives snuffed out by violent acts of crime. I had earned college and graduate degrees in religion and theology. However, an awareness of these apparent contradictions had never driven me to question God's justice and fairness. Romans 8:28 had always been my defense when confronted with such contradictory circumstances. Even though I could not explain the tragedies, I assumed that God had His own purposes for allowing people to suffer. But now my own mother's suffering forced new questions upon me. I had to have better answers. How could I say that my mother's suffering was God's will and would bring her good?

Can anyone who has heard the names Auschwitz and Dachai, or stood by the coffin of a loved one cut down by cancer, a heart attack, or a stroke, legitimately answer the question of the world's suffering by quoting Romans 8:28 and claiming that all this suffering works for the good of everyone who loves God, and reflects God's providential will?

It sounds too much like pious fluff and contradicts every scrap of evidence common to human experience. This answer may appear comforting to those prospering and in good health, but what happens when the hammer of suffering, disease, and death falls on them and destroys their happiness and health or that of a loved one?

If God "allowed" the Nazi slaughter of the Jews, how is He any different from the Nazi officers who passed the orders on and claimed as their defense that they were "just following orders"? If God isn't responsible, then why not? The Allied powers hanged people as war criminals for what they allowed to happen. We even have laws now that hold people civilly, and in some cases criminally, responsible for failing to render aid when they could have done so.

CHRIST'S VIEW OF GOD'S WATCHCARE

It is everywhere apparent in Christ's life that He believed in God's watchcare over His children. Possibly the best example of His trust in His Father's leading in His life is His Gethsemane prayer in which He asked that the cup of suffering on the cross pass from Him. He added, however, "Yet not as I will, but as you will" (Matt. 26:39, NIV). Faith in God's loving care is unmistakable in Christ's life and teaching. In the Sermon on the Mount, Christ points to God's watchcare over the birds of the air and the lilies of the field as examples of divine care for His children.

The Scriptures clearly state that God's will aims at human well-being on all levels. God's will is to help, heal, liberate, and save. God desires that human beings have life, joy, freedom, peace, and salvation. Consequently, God works through all our experiences to achieve this objective. Absolutely nothing happens to us outside of God's all-knowing and benevolent will, care, and concern. There are no exceptions!

However, we must not allow God to appear to approve, sanction, or to participate actively in the evil that befalls us. We cannot make God into a cosmic puppeteer who jerks people around for some sublime reason that we can understand only in the "sweet by and by." If we are to argue seriously that everything that happens to us—the good, the bad, and the ugly—comes from God by design, then why should Christians do anything to combat injustice, relieve sickness, or comfort the afflicted? That would be to go against divine will.

Unfortunately, many Christians apparently do believe this way, although they would wince if it were put to them this bluntly. As a consequence, they are passively indifferent to human pain and suffering. In the past Christians have used the Bible to justify the suffering of slavery, sexism, classism, etc. If it is simplistically true that no evil can befall "the righteous," then suffering people are clearly unrighteous, getting their own just deserts, and we should celebrate their suffering, not combat it or comfort them in it. After all, it is God's will for them to suffer.

This approach portrays God as being above all moral and ethical considerations, actively using evil means to bring about His purposes. How then do we square the promise of God's care for us with the crushing tragedies that often bend and break His chosen ones? We can begin by understanding God's primary goal for His children in this life.

WHAT IS THE GOOD GOD WOULD DO FOR US IN THIS LIFE?

We can best understand Romans 8:28 in the context of verse 29, which suggests that God is working all things together for the purpose of conforming His children to the likeness of His Son, Jesus Christ. The text claims that God works all things together for the ultimate good purpose of making us like Christ. The good that God has in mind is to pattern us after Christ, not to play the role of a cosmic Santa Claus. Certainly, Scripture does promise a degree of physical and material prosperity in this life. However, these blessings are to be realized fully only in the future temporal kingdom established at the second coming of Christ. Today Christ is establishing a spiritual kingdom. The primary rewards of this life are love, joy, wisdom, and peace.

In this context we can make sense of both life's sweet and life's bitter experiences. God is not the source of suffering and evil, but neither does He protect His followers from every tragedy. Yet God comforts and sustains us in them, working with us in the suffering to accomplish His purpose of conforming us more fully to Christ and of achieving His ultimate purposes for His people.

Joseph's story is a wonderful illustration of this transcendent truth. It is a concrete example of human suffering from injustice redeemed by a faith-filled human response that enabled God to bless Joseph and his family, and to work wonderfully to accomplish His ultimate purposes.

DEFINING EVIL

Some argue that God will never use evil to bring about good. What they mean is that He never uses suffering and pain to accomplish His ends. Evil is something demeaning and destructive, wounding and never healing. Thus its end is death and not life. It is difficult for a technologically oriented culture to find meaning in suffering. An antitheistic worldview provides no framework for dealing with pain and suffering. But that is not to say suffering has no meaning in it.

Can a spanking given to a child be defined as evil? It certainly is painful. But few would agree that it is evil. Is the surgical removal of a gallbladder evil? After all, the surgery does bring pain.

Christianity Today featured an article entitled "And God Made Pain." I agree with the article's view of pain as one of the most remarkable design features of the human body. The author pointed out that if we would only listen, pain often makes us aware that we are abusing our brains, our eyes, our stomachs, our feet, and even our backs. He writes, "I wish people would cease seeing pain as something to avoid at all costs. If we would, our lives would not only be richer, but our bodies would be healthier."[2] Viewing pain in this light enables us to understand that it is not necessarily evil. It helps us to recognize that God originally intended pain to keep us healthy. Once sin came, God used pain to help the healing process. A third function of pain brings us a sense of dependence on God, thus making us more like Christ.

RECOGNIZE THAT NOT EVERYTHING IS GOD'S WILL

Acknowledging God's omnipotence, we may in a general sense say that God allows suffering. If He chose to stop suffering, He certainly could. However, we must be careful not to make God responsible for suffering.

Suffering appears to be random, chaotic, meaningless, and tawdry, striking the good and the bad with equal force and destructiveness. It seems ultimately absurd, driving people to insanity at many different levels.

One Christian I know graphically expresses his own response to these evil paradoxes in his life. "Life is complicated right now. . . . Like everybody else, I occasionally get sulky, testy, prickly. It's hard to keep your balance when people try to rip your head off. It's mind-numbing to have people lie about me, trying to turn my life into a caricature. But when all is said and done, beyond all the conflicts and hurt feelings and wounded soul, I know God is good, He is with me, for me, on my side, trying to help me."

LET GOD BE GOD

Recognizing that human beings cannot always understand God's actions can help us cope with suffering. Since we cannot see the whole picture, it is difficult for us to understand what He is doing. The honest Christian will admit that we do not have all the answers.

A vibrant and vigorous Christian life cannot survive without faith assumptions. There are realities that we cannot deny without undermining the basic principles of Christianity and crippling our faith. These include but are not limited to the fact that the omnipotent, all-powerful God is always in control of all the affairs of His universe, that God possesses all wisdom coupled with righteousness and holiness, and that He is a loving God who always works for the good of His creatures. While we do not believe that God is responsible for suffering, neither can we say that suffering happens outside of God's will. To believe that pictures a God who is not in control of His universe.

A dynamic faith depends on a deep reverence for God. God is accountable to no one and owes no explanation for His actions. Always insisting on explicit answers to life's paradoxes will result in creeping bitterness toward Him and life. For the time being we must continue our spiritual journey by trusting God in the midst of the mysterious, "storing away our questions for a lengthy conversation on the other side." Despite all that, however, some suffering can be explained.

SUFFERING RESULTS FROM HUMAN FREEDOM

A loving God who desires a free response of love from us requires that we be created with the freedom to choose. Consequently, a biblical understanding of suffering takes human freedom seriously. God gives us the ability to reject His counsel, to disobey the moral or physical laws that govern our health and happiness. And He does not necessarily shield us from the evil results. Paul counseled, "Whatsoever a man soweth, that shall he also reap" (Gal. 6:7). If I choose to smoke, God will not work a miracle to keep me from getting cancer. Nor will He necessarily protect me from lung disease even if I do not smoke but work around others who do. Should we decide to walk out in front of a speeding automobile, ordinarily God will not intervene to save us from the consequences.

Our suffering can result from the evil seeds that others have sown. The physical, emotional, or even mental weakness of our parents or our grandparents often causes our suffering. We may inherit a predisposition to a certain disease. God's grace doesn't always reverse those genetic conditions. He had nothing to do with my mother's Alzheimer's. Her suffering resulted from inherited bad genes.

The actions of friends, of people we do not know, or even our enemies can bring us suffering. A drunken driver veers across the median. A crushing head-on collision smashes the face and severely damages the brain of the wife and mother of three children.

A businessman is unjustly accused of murdering a partner, then is wrongly convicted of the crime and sentenced to life in prison.

While there are no good answers as to the why these mind-tangling things happen, faith sustains us and reminds us that there is more to the story.

THE REST OF THE STORY

The purpose of God's watchcare is to preserve life for not only the present, but most of all for eternity (John 10:10). It seeks to maintain not only length of life, but its quality and richness. Unfortunately, this purpose does not always make itself plain from day to day. Tragedies happen that seem to have no point whatever and to contribute nothing to life's total plan and purpose. But we must always remember that there is more to come, that the story is not yet over, that there is still another chapter. In the same way, Christians cannot say that any single event in their life lacks purpose. The truth is that the purpose will be revealed later on. Jesus taught this lesson when He said: "What I do thou knowest not now" (John 13:7).

On Good Friday the cross must have seemed the most purposeless event in the history of humanity. Only as the story of redeemed humanity developed, only in the succeeding chapters, did its purpose begin to reveal itself. As time went on, it became more and more evident that on the cross, as in no other event, God went before us to preserve life. It is therefore in retrospect that we are most often likely to see God's purpose made unmistakably plain in a pattern that gradually emerges out of the events.

A young man studying for the ministry was dangerously ill for a year. At that time the illness seemed to be nothing but a miserable interruption and hindrance to the main goal of his life. After many years in the ministry, however, he recognized the period of illness for what it really was—a valuable part of the man's preparation for the pastoral ministry of the church.

God's promises assure us that even though hard times come to us, He offers us all the grace we need or can handle, thus enabling us ultimately to rise above our suffering and to experience God's peace and grace in our lives.

TRUST IN GOD

Faith and trust in God can bring great solace, comfort, and hope to God's children. When believers accept this truth, and the light of God's loving care illuminates the mind, they are set free from much unnecessary fear and anxiety. Their source of joy and strength is their knowledge that their heavenly Father rules by His authority and will allow nothing to befall believers that will separate them from His love. Christians believe that they have been received into God's safekeeping and entrusted to the care of the angels. Even though they pass through the water and the fire, no evil or harm can hinder God's work of making them like Christ. Nothing can separate them from Christ or call into question their future life with God (Isa. 43:1-3).

This hope sustained the prophets. They repeated this assurance and expressed this joy and comfort often. In Psalm 118:6, David says: "The Lord is on my side." Psalm 27:1: "The Lord is the strength of my life; of whom shall I be afraid?" The believer need not fear even the approach of death (Ps. 23:4). Psalm 56:4 promises: "In God (I will praise His word), in God I have put my trust; I will not fear. What can flesh do to me?" (NKJV).

The life of those who trust God will be very different from that of those who deny His love and care. New power and purpose will fill them, because they know God works with them. They see, even in their suffering, new potentialities based on their submission to God and their ability to seize and use those circumstances. Hospital visitation led me into a room where two men were expected to die. One of them, a devout Christian, was quietly praying. The voice of the other polluted the air with swearing and cursing.

Trust in God makes Christians unique in the world, enabling them to witness to their faith in God and their love for others. When unjustly hurt by someone else, Christians are able to overlook this evil. They find the strength to turn their thoughts to God and believe that despite whatever acts the enemy has wickedly committed against them, God's love guarantees ultimate victory.

NO FAILURE WITH GOD

The promises of God are forceful enough to prevent ultimate failure (Isa. 43:1-3). God's plan may have many setbacks, but He never gives up (Heb. 13:5). Sometimes He can rebuild a life by employing the scraps that men and women leave behind—their blunders, their stakes, and their crosses. God can use a foolish family feud like the one in the story of Joseph to carry His purpose forward (Gen. 45). An exile, an imprisonment, a dark night, a miserable failure—all these things He can rearrange and weave into the pattern of His plan. God does not deliberately bring about war, but He can use its scrap material to carry out His grand strategy. Though in later years my mother suffered with Alzheimer's, her life was still a great success. God used her to educate two preachers, one church school teacher, and two other children who are contributing to God's work as active laypeople.

Trust is the bottom line in Christianity. "Faith is the assurance of things hoped for, the conviction of things not seen" (Heb. 11:1, RSV). If we walked by sight, we might understand everything. However, then we would not need faith. Faith enables us to transcend the tragedies, to persevere amid the paradoxes. We can square what is with what will be, knowing, as William Johnsson writes in his paraphrase of Romans

8:28: "He [God] works all things together for the good of those who love Him."[4]

---

[1] H. S. Kushner, *When Bad Things Happen to Good People,* p. 29.

[2] Paul Brand and Philip Yancey, "And God Made Pain," *Christianity Today,* Jan. 10, 1994, p. 20.

[3] James Dobson, *When God Doesn't Make Sense* (Wheaton, Ill.: Tyndale House, 1993), p. 58.

[4] William Johnsson, in *Adventist Review,* Feb. 24, 1994, p. 4.

- CHAPTER 13 -

THE SLIPPERY
SLOPE OF DOUBT

CHRISTIANITY IS PROPERLY CONFESSIONAL, THAT IT IS ABSOLUTELY TRUE, WAS
NOT DOUBTED BY CATHOLIC OR PROTESTANT UNTIL QUITE RECENTLY. . . . IT WAS SEEN
AS AN UNCHANGING GOSPEL, HANDED DOWN BY PEN AND MOUTH FROM AGE TO AGE,
GENERATION TO GENERATION, MOTHER TO CHILD, TEACHER TO TAUGHT, PULPIT TO PEW
. . . THAT WHICH HAS BEEN BELIEVED IN EVERY PLACE, IN EVERY CENTURY, BY ALL
CHRISTIAN MEN AND WOMEN.[1]

—DAVID B. WELLS

The privilege of being reared and educated in a conservative Christian environment was not enough. Ron Numbers attended Christian schools from the first grade through college. Later he earned a Ph.D. at the University of California at Berkeley. During his graduate studies he agonized over the conflict between the conclusions of science as opposed to the teachings of Scripture. After months of struggle, he finally "decided to follow science rather than Scripture."[2] With the following cryptic words he describes his own journey into unbelief: "I quickly, though not painlessly, slid down the proverbial slippery slope toward unbelief."[3]

In 1982 the Louisiana creation/evolution trial requested his services as a possible expert witness. Wendall R. Byrd, the creationist lawyer, tried to recruit him for his side of the debate. After two lengthy sessions probing Numbers' historical knowledge and Christian commitment, Byrd labeled Ron "an agnostic."[4] With some discomfort, Ron accepted that label. He writes: "The tag still feels foreign and uncomfortable, but it accurately reflects my theological uncertainty."[5]

Most experience doubt—even great spiritual and theological leaders. But not all slide into deep doubt, as did Ron Numbers.

SPURGEON'S BATTLE WITH DOUBT

Charles H. Spurgeon, the great English preacher, experienced a period when doubt threatened his mind and soul. He writes: "There was an evil hour when I slipped the anchor of my faith; I cut the cable of my belief; I no longer moored myself hard by the coasts of Revelation; I allowed my vessel to drift before the wind; I said to reason, 'Be thou my captain'; I said to my own brain, 'Be thou my rudder'; and I started on my mad voyage."[6]

"I went on, and as I went, the skies were brilliant with coruscations of brilliancy. I saw sparks flying upward that pleased me, and I thought, 'If this be free thought, it is a happy thing.' My thoughts seemed gems, and I scattered stars with my hands; but anon, instead of these coruscations of glory, I saw grim fiends, fierce and horrible, start up from the waters, and as I dashed on, they gnashed their teeth, and grinned upon me: they seized the prow of my ship and dragged me on, while I, in part gloried at the rapidity of my motion, but yet shuddered at the terrible rate with which I passed the old landmarks of my faith.

"As I hurried forward, with an awful speed, I began to doubt my very existence: I doubted if there was a world, I doubted if there were such a thing as myself. I went to the very verge of the dreary realms of unbelief. I went to the very bottom of the sea of infidelity. I doubted everything."[7]

However, for Spurgeon the very experience of doubt shook him to the core of his being. While fearfully pondering the validity of doubt, he heard a voice, as it were, saying, "And can this doubt be true?" Seeing that the principle of doubt alters the very soil that nurtures the roots of Christianity and even reality, he immediately rejected doubt's suggestions. Faith then reasserted itself and steered him back to the realism of Scripture.

His reaffirmation of faith in the Scriptures follows: "Oh, Book of books! And wast thou written by my God! Then I bow before thou book of vast authority! Thou art a proclamation from the Emperor of heaven: far be it from me to exercise my reason in contradiction to thee. Reason, thy place is to stand and find out what this volume means, not to tell what this book ought to say. Come thou, my reason, my intellect, sit thou down and listen, for these words are the word of God."[8]

Never again did Spurgeon surrender to doubt. "Ask me again to be an infidel? No! I have tried it; it was sweet at first, but bitter afterwards. Now, lashed to God's gospel more firmly than ever, standing as on a rock of adamant, I defy the arguments of hell to move me; for I know in whom I have believed, and am persuaded that he is able to keep that which I have committed unto him."[9] Spurgeon remained a faithful preacher of God's Word until his death in 1892.

G. CAMPBELL MORGAN'S TRIAL OF FAITH

Debilitating attacks of doubt interrupted the ministry of G. Campbell Morgan, another great preacher and expositor of Scripture, for a full two-year period. Under the training of his father, a deep student of the Bible and a powerful preacher himself, Campbell Morgan's ministry began at age 13. During his theological studies he came under the influence of Darwin, Huxley, Spencer, and others, whose philosophy cast a gloomy shadow over the early twentieth-century religious world. Consequently, Morgan experienced a "partial eclipse of faith" and had to face the "specters of the mind."[10]

For two years he floundered, debating in the "secularist halls" the issues presented by the evolutionist philosophers. "There came a moment when I was sure of nothing," he confessed.[11]

The real crisis came when he realized his total lack of faith that the Bible was the inspired Word of God. He immediately canceled all preaching engagements. Then taking all his books, both those attacking and those defending the Bible, he put them all in a bookcase. Often he told the story of how he met this crisis. Relating the deep emotions he felt as he turned the key in the lock of the door of the bookcase, he said, "I can hear the click of that lock now."[12]

Then he went down to the bookstore and bought a new Bible. As he began to study, he said to himself, "I am no longer sure that this is what my father claims it to be—the Word of God. But of this I *am* sure. If it *be* the Word of God, and if I come to it with an unprejudiced and open mind, it will bring assurance to my soul of itself."[13] What happened? "That Bible *found* me," Morgan said. "I began to read and study it then, in 1883. I have been a student ever since, and I still am [in 1938]."[14] Anyone who has read Morgan's book *The Triumph of Faith* knows the depth of his faith and that his faith held strong until his death.

BILLY GRAHAM'S DUEL WITH DOUBT

No one is safe from the poisonous fangs of doubt, not even the greatest evangelist of modern time. Billy Graham stepped unintentionally onto the slippery slope of doubt in 1948. He had just been invited to conduct his first major citywide crusade in Los Angeles, California, to begin in late 1949. Because Graham was in the thick of a disturbing conflict of faith at the time that the committee accepted his conditions, he was almost sorry to receive the request.

Charles Templeton, a close friend of Graham's, had for some time harbored doubts about the integrity of the Bible. Hoping to understand the nature of inspiration better, Templeton decided to enter Princeton Theological Seminary. Graham also craved for postgraduate studies. During Templeton's first year at Princeton, Graham and Templeton often spent hours in debate and prayer. Templeton's doubts about Scripture intensified, and the more Graham read and debated, the more confused he became. Yet he could not accept Chuck's position that a doctrine of biblical infallibility was intellectually untenable. To Templeton, Graham was a surface thinker unwilling to explore the implications of his position.

In June the Billy Graham evangelistic team held a 10-day campaign at the railroad city of Altoona, in the heart of the Allegheny Mountains in Pennsylvania, which Grady Wilson called "the greatest flop we've ever had anywhere." [15] Local preparation had been scanty, and the ministers were at one another's throats.

Graham believed the cause of the failure lay in himself, in his nagging uncertainty. Perhaps, after all, Templeton was right to insist, "Billy, your faith is too simple. You'll have to get a new jargon if you want to communicate to this generation." [16]

One evening during a serious discussion with Graham, a mutual friend mentioned a remark that he said Templeton had made an hour or two earlier. He reportedly said, "Poor Billy. If he goes on the way he's going, he'll never do anything for God. He'll be circumscribed to a small little narrow interpretation of the Bible, and his ministry will be curtailed. As for me, I'm taking a different road." [17]

The comment deeply disturbed and hurt Graham. After supper, instead of attending evening service, he retired to his log cabin and read again the Bible passages concerning its authority. He recalled someone saying that the prophets used such phrases as "The Word of the Lord came . . ." or "Thus saith the Lord . . ." more than 2,000 times. He meditated on the attitude of Christ, who fulfilled the law of the prophets: "He loved the Scriptures, quoted from them constantly, and never once intimated that they might be wrong."

Then he went out into the forest and wandered up the mountainside, praying as he walked, "Lord, what shall I do? What shall be the direction of my life?" He had reached what he believed to be a crisis.

He saw that faith is often based on evidence and not always demonstration, as are many scientific truths. Graham thought of the faith used constantly in daily life. For example, he did not know how a train or a plane or a car worked, but he rode them. Nor did he know why a brown cow could eat green grass and yield white milk, but he drank milk. Was it only in things of the Spirit that such faith was wrong?

Returning to his room, he got his Bible, then went out into the night. His own words graphically picture his victory over doubt: "I got to a stump and put the Bible on the stump, and knelt down, and I said, 'O God, I cannot prove certain things. I cannot answer some of the questions Chuck is raising and some of the other people are raising, but I accept this Book by faith as the Word of God.'" [18]

From this experience Billy Graham went on to the Los Angeles crusade, where the greatest evangelistic ministry in modern times was born out of faith in, and the preaching of, the Word of God. Few would question that the success of his ministry can be attributed to Graham's bedrock faith in the authority of God's Word and his proclamation of that Word.

IS DOUBT SIN?

Certainly not. Any thinking person will, as they struggle with the great issues that we face in our modern world, experience doubt. In fact, a well-known author says that faith grows stronger in conflict with doubt. [19] Consequently, we should not despair when we have doubt and question the reliability of Scripture.

WHY DOUBT IS UNREASONABLE

Following are some reasons for not allowing doubt to destroy our faith. The first most serious fallacy of modern thought is the widespread notion that biblical truth does not square with true science; therefore, the doctrine of biblical inspiration is untenable to a committed scientist or to any serious thinking person. An educated person may be able to accept the spiritual teachings of the Bible, but never its scientific and historical teachings. Billy Graham struggled with this concept.

However, the statements and teachings of hundreds of scientists disprove both of the above statements. Isaac Newton (1642-1727), famous for his discovery of the law of universal gravitation, was a man of gigantic intellect, a scientist, but also a genuine believer in Christ as his Saviour, and in the authority of the Bible. Not only well known for his writings on the accuracy of the prophetic teachings of the Bible, Newton defended the Genesis story of Creation, the biblical chronology, and the biblical account of the Flood. He believed in the six-day creation record, and said, "We account the Scriptures of God to be the most sublime philosophy. I find more sure marks of authenticity in the Bible than in any profane history whatever."[20]

In 1864 in London 717 scientists signed a remarkable manifesto entitled "The Declaration of Students of the Natural and Physical Sciences." It affirmed their confidence in the scientific integrity of Holy Scripture. The list who signed this declaration included 86 fellows of the Royal Society and many other prominent scientists of the nineteenth century.[21]

Today we find thousands of unashamed scientists, literal creationists, who believe that God created all things in the six solar days described in the first chapter of Genesis.

Many groups and societies of scientists hold to the biblical story of Creation. One of the most significant is the Creation Research Society. Organized in 1963 by 10 scientists, it soon grew to a membership of more than 700. The members of this scientific society have at least one postgraduate degree. More than 2,000 other sustaining members are also scientists. All members who belong to this society embrace the inspiration of the Bible, the substitutionary atonement of Christ, and the historicity of the Genesis record of a special six-day Creation and worldwide cataclysmic flood.[22]

True science, then, as opposed to what Paul referred to as the "profane and vain babblings and oppositions of science falsely so called" (1 Tim. 6:20), leads us to God. It results in a greater faith in the

131

Scriptures and establishes clearly the validity of the scientific teachings of Scripture itself.

The second reason Christians can be just as confident of what they believe as the scientist is the fact that the truth claims of both Christianity and science rest on similar assumptions.

Leonard R. Brand, professor of biology at Loma Linda University, points out that both Christian perspectives and the nonbiblical perspectives of science share similar presuppositions. Both, he argues, are "made on the basis of faith."[23] According to Brand, where we posit our faith will dictate what we believe. Those who have more faith in antitheistic scientific theories than in a Christian view of science will likely conclude that conflicting scientific dating methods "are accurate."[24] On the other hand, those whose faith in a Christian worldview is stronger than their faith in secular scientific theories will be convinced that current dating methods of fossils, rocks, etc., "are not correct."[25]

Many acknowledge today that both natural science and social science always operate within a framework of assumptions. We take either a theistic assumption or an antitheistic one. A person with faith in the God of the Bible begins with the biblical assumption that God is the Creator of all things. The Christian also presupposes that the Scriptures are a revelation of God and are fully trustworthy. When it comes to the origin and nature of human beings, the earth, etc., both a Christian view of science and a non-Christian view have evidence to support their beliefs. But neither can demonstrate or prove their beliefs to be true. One belief system is just as valid as the other given one's original assumptions.

A third reason for not doubting the truths of biblical Christianity is that much of the work of modern science is a purely human endeavor that leaves no room for the supernatural. It assumes that all we can know about reality can be discovered in observable phenomena. However, Christians recognize that we must believe in God and His Word in order to reason correctly in areas of science that cannot be proved true or false. To deny the reality of God and to reject the truths revealed in His Word and in nature are to set ourselves on a course that leads ultimately to the denial of the reality of a personal God and the historicity of the Genesis story of Creation.

If humanity is created by, and dependent upon, its Creator, then it follows that only in relationship to our Creator and a correlation of the evidences of Scripture and nature can we possibly come to correct conclusions about God's Creation.

Conversely, when we reject God and the revelation of Himself in Scripture, our assumptions change. We begin with no absolutes, no objective perimeters to guide us, and we assume that we are totally capable, through our own unaided research, reason, and logic, of discovering ultimate reality. This concept distorted the Enlightenment of the eighteenth century.

Growing out of the Enlightenment was a new construction of history based on an extended process that sees human beings as progressing from a religious stage in which authority answered questions, through a metaphysical stage in which philosophy ruled, to a positivist stage that accepts empirical investigation as the only reliable way to truth.

This approach takes an unwarranted high view of human intellect. In fact, human beings became the only authority. They can not only discover all truth but also determine and realize their own destiny. Modern philosophies see humanity as being fully responsible for its own destiny. Max Stackhouse agrees and states unequivocally that he has "full confidence in the ability of man technically and politically to shape his destiny."[26] But one has to ask, "Where is the proof for such an assumption?"

We could cite still other reasons that we should not allow the findings of modern secular science to destroy our faith in the time-tested truths of Christianity. Benjamin L. Clausen, a research scientist in the Geoscience Research Center, Loma Linda, California, points out that there is "more to reality than science can address."[27] He argues that since supernatural events are not presently observable or repeatable, science cannot speak authoritatively in those areas simply because they cannot put them in a laboratory and reproduce them to prove whether or not they are true.

Faith in the unseen realities revealed in Scripture provides additional information unavailable to science, thus giving the Christian reason to believe the teaching of the Bible. The element of faith is one of the reasons that Christians can, as Campbell Morgan claims, still believe in the Genesis story of Creation.[28]

Science is also limited in the area of moral and ethical questions.

It accepts only that which it can observe, and consequently it provides no absolute standard to guide humanity in dealing with the moral and ethical issues of life.

Possibly the most important reason for not making science our final authority is that science cannot satisfactorily answer the ultimate questions of life. Thus it fails to provide purpose and meaning to life.

HOW TO OVERCOME DOUBT

The first means that God has given us to overcome doubt is our experience in Christ. All three of the men discussed in this chapter were men who had deep religious lives. Experience in spiritual realities is the good soil in which an intelligent faith grows. Even though our minds may see conflicts between the revelation of God and science, an honest person will be slow to jump to conclusions. When doubt disturbed them to the point that they could no longer effectively preach the Word of God, the memory of their personal experience with God kept them steady until they could investigate and resolve the issues raised by doubt.

Second, they all turned to the Scriptures to overcome their doubt and to rebuild their faith. Their study of the Scriptures provided an intelligent and informed faith that enabled the men to see the hidden harmony between science and revelation. The Bible is a living book and thus is self-authenticating. It carries its own credentials and holds within itself the seeds of faith that if nurtured will blossom full-blown in the life of the one reading the Word.

Jesus said, "The words that I speak unto you, they are spirit, and they are life" (John 6:63). The creative energy that called the worlds into existence is in the Word of God. This Word imparts power and begets life. Every command is a promise that, if accepted by the will and received into the soul, will bring with it the life of the infinite One. "It transforms the nature and re-creates the soul in the image of God." [29] Not only are the difficult questions raised by doubt answered adequately, but the darkness that shadows the soul lifts and a joyous certainty fills the heart and life.

Third, all three resolved their doubts in the context of ministry to others. The fact that doubt frustrated the ministry of Spurgeon, Morgan, and Graham unmasked the destructive nature of doubt itself.

Overcoming this doubt was the only road to fulfilling their call to ministry and effectively sharing the Word of God. For these three great men, doing their ministry involved a renewed study of the Scriptures in preparation for serving others. This renewed study of the Bible, coupled with the proclamation of the Word of God, resulted not only in the conversion of many individuals but also in renewal of their own souls and the enlargement of their own minds to see the validity of Scripture truths regarding science. Consequently, this renewal in their own lives as well as in those of their hearers worked effectively to overcome the doubts that had previously threatened to undermine their faith.

Experience, Bible study, and ministry are the three interconnected realities that build and preserve our faith. Even if we accidentally find ourselves on the slippery slope of doubt, these three undergirding realities are more than able to break our fall, reanchor our faith, and help us rebuild an even stronger faith than we had previously.

---

[1] D. B. Wells, *No Place for Truth,* pp. 104, 105.

[2] Ronald L. Numbers, *The Creationist, the Evolution of Scientific Creationism* (Berkeley, Calif.: University of California Press, 1992), p. xvi.

[3] *Ibid.*

[4] *Ibid.*

[5] *Ibid.*

[6] Charles H. Spurgeon, "The Bible, the Word of God," *The Present Truth* 9, No. 1: 1.

[7] *Ibid.*

[8] *Ibid.*

[9] *Ibid.*

[10] G. Campbell Morgan, *The Ministry of the Word* (London: Fleming H. Revell Co., 1919), p. 15.

[11] Harold Calkins, *Master Preachers* (Washington, D.C.: Review and Herald Pub. Assn., 1960), p. 59.

[12] *Ibid.*

[13] *Ibid.*

[14] *Ibid.*

[15] John Pollock, *Billy Graham* (New York: McGraw-Hill, 1966), p. 52.

[16] *Ibid.*

[17] *Ibid.,* p. 53.

[18] *Ibid.*

[19] Ellen G. White, *Testimonies for the Church* (Mountain View, Calif.: Pacific Press Pub. Assn., 1948), vol. 4, p. 117.

[20] Henry M. Morris, *Men of Science, Men of God* (El Cajon, Calif.: Master Books, 1988), p. 28.

[21] *Ibid.,* p. 75.

[22] *Ibid.,* pp. 94, 95.

[23] Leonard R. Brand, "Resolving the Conflict Between Science and Religion," *Liberty,* January/February 1990, p. 27.

[24] *Ibid.*

[25] *Ibid.*

[26] M. L. Stackhouse, *Ethics and the Urban Ethos,* p. 15.

[27] Benjamin L. Clausen, "Can Science Explain It All?" *Dialogue,* No. 2 (1991): 8.

[28] G. Campbell Morgan, *The Triumph of Faith* (Old Tappan, N.J.: Fleming H. Revell Co., 1944), p. 39.

[29] E. G. White, *Education,* p. 126.